Wakefield Press

THE DECLINE
OF THE TEA LADY

T0358142

THE
DECLINE
OF THE
TEA LADY

Management for dissidents

JENNY STEWART

**Wakefield
Press**

AUTHOR'S NOTE

My thanks to *Quadrant* magazine, in which versions of many of these pieces first appeared.

Wakefield Press
1 The Parade West
Kent Town
South Australia 5067
www.wakefieldpress.com.au

First published 2004
Reprinted 2004

Cover designed by Liz Nicholson, designBITE
Designed and typeset by Clinton Ellicott, Wakefield Press
Printed and bound by Hyde Park Press

National Library of Australia
Cataloguing-in-publication entry

Stewart, Jenny, 1950–   .
The decline of the tea lady: management for dissidents.

ISBN 1 86254 611 8.

1. Australian essays – 21st century. 2. Corporate culture.
3. Organizational behavior. I. Title.

A824.4

FOR MY MOTHER

CONTENTS

Foreword by Jack Waterford   IX

Introduction   1

The world of blah   5

The cult of management and the
decline of the tea lady   17

How to get on   27

Take me to your leader   39

Letter from academia   51

It's academic   59

Dismantling the state   72

The man in the grey cardigan   84

The politics of place   99

Volunteering   115

Confessions of a bush treasurer   126

Do you mind?   139

This feminist thing   155

Speaking out   170

The Americans, Mate   182

FOREWORD

This is a delightful book. It is also subversive, but in the best possible way. It is imbued with the sense of purpose – indeed, in many cases, the higher purpose – of the state, the bureaucracy, the agency, and even informal organisations in business and community affairs, while showing that sometimes that purpose is misunderstood, occasionally it is frustrated and very often we do not achieve what we have set out to do, because of the ways in which we have adapted, or failed to adapt, to changing circumstance.

Jenny Stewart's anecdotes, explanations and description of the machinery of society in action could hardly fail to underline the fact that the system does not work as well as it might and to invite some cynicism about where we might end up, but she, clearly, believes not only in the journey but in the idea that if we put our mind to the mechanics we might be able to stumble through.

Talking about such things, weighing such changes, and asking such questions is by no means new. All too often, however, too many of the books and articles describing or agonising about the society we have been, now are, or are becoming, while certainly earnest, learned and even incisive, are almost unreadable. Jenny Stewart's book does not depend on abstract nouns, character-forming citations or that general shortage of full stops which represents a greater threat to human comfort than the disappearing hydrocarbon. Rather it makes its point by anecdote and illustration, and by the creation of images, from the tea-lady we all remember, the world of blah and guru, of quiz show and of volunteers and bureaucracies big and small. It's all the more powerful for that.

Jack Waterford
Editor in Chief
The Canberra Times

INTRODUCTION

There is a story about an old lady who was asked by her grandson, a physicist, what she thought were the origins of the universe.

Well, she said, she thought the universe was supported on the back of a very large turtle.

'But grandmother,' her grandson replied, 'what does the turtle rest on?'

His grandmother thought for a while. 'I guess,' she said, 'it is turtles all the way down.'

I feel the same about organisations. They are people both all the way down and, more to the point, people all the way up. That's what makes them so fascinating.

For years I assumed that, in general, the people at the top knew what they were doing. They had the best advice, the most experience, the keenest insights. Then, gradually, I began to realise that most in fact had no idea what they were doing, but unlike more cautious and no doubt ineffectual folk, they were prepared at least to make decisions. They were put in their jobs to do things no one else wanted to do. In a way, leadership was the most menial task of all.

At this point, I began to consult the vast and rather grim literature which purports to tell people how to run organisations. I could see little there that I recognised. Organisations were supposed to be rational, yet I have never known an organisation – business, university, public service, volunteer – which was not a seething mass of more-or-less incompatible personal agendas, held together only by really poor communication.

This is why most organisations have an air of barely concealed lunacy about them. It is quite bracing, once you get the hang of it. Consultants come and go, and reports are produced. There are meetings, crises and urgent summonses. Visitors appear for no apparent reason. What do they want? Who knows? What is going on behind the smiling countenances? Who cares? They are here, which means we must be here, too.

If you keep out of the way, and don't take any of it too seriously, there is comic opera all around you. Slightly more dangerous, depending upon where you are, is to ask questions. Although I wouldn't call myself a particularly brave person, scepticism comes naturally to me. So many people are trying to make us believe in their own estimation of themselves, or in some product, service or idea they happen to be pushing, that asking questions becomes, to alter one of Lady Bracknell's lines, not just a pleasure but a duty.

If you keep asking questions, answers start to accumulate, rarely in answer to the original questions, but as a sort of running commentary on the things that happen around you. In my case these thoughts started gradually to accumulate, on bits of paper, in exercise books, in erratically kept diaries. Out of them grew the essays in this book.

Working life is not a common subject for essays, which in the Australian context at least, tend to be either political or literary. In any case, writers are too busy being writers to do other things, and the people doing the other things rarely become writers. That leaves the field to the sociologists and the management consultants. But it is much too important a subject to leave to them. People need work, and tend to behave strangely when they are deprived of it (such as volunteering to look after their grandchildren). It is the organisations we work for that give us credibility and a degree of confidence. Even if we are not very proud of them, or they of us, the people we have met through them, the situations weathered, the good times that would probably be unrecognisable if we could re-live them intact, continue to haunt us.

But that still leaves the question as to how seriously, at the personal level, to take the business of business? Not many epitaphs read 'he made a lot of money', or 'she was good at her job'. As far as maintaining personal equilibrium is concerned, it helps if we can see through the façade while still believing in it.

Or perhaps, having seen through the façade, it is impossible to believe in it and we must simply carry on stoically. At least, we say to ourselves, we have a job. Most of the world's population would eagerly trade their opportunities for our problems. But still, niggling away somewhere is the little, insistent, tinny melody of 'might have been'. A little more luck, a bit more nerve and – who knows?

After a time Cassandra's curse is everyone's. Just as we have become wise, so has the world become less inclined to listen to us. But then, having seen it all before, we can afford a little irony. As someone said, experience is recognising your mistakes when you make them all over again.

You will have gathered by now that this is not a book for the movers and shakers, the ambitious or the driven. It is not for those who have 'made it', or even those who wish they had. It is for those who got off the bus to enjoy the view, or who, like me, could never work out where the bus was leaving from in the first place. It is for all of us who don't need the expense account, the hype or the silly mantras and who now, rather wickedly, are beginning to enjoy being left behind. Perhaps it's time we got to know each other. Perhaps the really interesting people are not on the bus, after all.

THE WORLD OF BLAH

A friend was reporting a recent meeting at her company, at which the boss was justifying his decision to get rid of a number of employees.

'So, what did he say?' I asked. 'Oh, you know, rightsizing and restructuring, the inevitability of change, how we need to work together – the usual blah.'

I am sure you know the world of blah. Blah is a particular way in which we appear to be talking to each other, while not actually communicating anything. It is a form of verbal muzak, in which nothing surprises, nothing explains. Words do their duty, no more, no less. It is one of the many ways we have for explaining things we have not really thought about, for obscuring the real reasons for our actions and, beyond that, for filling in the silence that terrifies us so much.

We all do it, because in our culture it is accounted far more blessed to transmit than to receive. Consider the management conference, the epicentre of blah. People who speak at conferences are generally paid to do so, while those who are expected to listen and then ask questions (a much more difficult task) must pay for the privilege. I suppose that is why the audience always subsides gratefully into the arms of morning tea and can only with difficulty be harassed back into the conference room.

People on podiums so frequently abuse their privilege of taking up other people's time, it is a wonder conference organisers get anyone at all to come along. Admittedly, hardly anyone is paying for their registration themselves, and the Truly Important either don't show up or don't stay long. But there must be other factors at work to explain why so many people, apparently voluntarily, subject themselves to other people's recycled verbal leftovers. Giles Auty, the art critic, reckons that we Australians are brought up on clumsy, predictable and overly long speeches, and expect to be bored on public occasions. Perhaps this is why conferences remain popular. Or perhaps, boring as they are, they are still to be preferred to another day at the office.

We have devised many institutions for wasting each other's time: the schools and universities crammed with kids who would be better off in the workforce; the Parliament, which comes to life only when members get the chance to try to embarrass each other in question time; and the hundreds of thousands of committee meetings, up and down the country, where people sit in their places, doodling and wishing someone, somehow, would make a decision.

Wherever people are given air time because of who they are, rather than because they might have something to say, we run the risk of encouraging blah. To be confident of the diagnosis, try these simple tests. If you habitually attend meetings at which everyone repeats what they said last time, you are probably in a blah zone. At conferences, workshops, seminars and focus groups certain words, such as 'information economy', 'globalisation', 'stakeholder' and 'empowerment', are virtually infallible indicators of blah, as are the inseparable twins, 'efficiency and effectiveness'.

It is not that these terms are meaningless, but rather that they are employed to convey a vague portentousness, rather than any real conceptual sense. They are a way of avoiding discussion, while appearing to promote it. Unlike jargon, which proclaims exclusion, blah is half-understood by just about everyone. It is a kind of lingua franca of the media age.

Blah is not new, because there have always been people who take up a lot of airtime while saying very little. But there is more of it about than ever before. In societies which have become more complex, but in which average human capacity has not notably increased, there are relatively fewer people who actually know what they are talking about. Those who half-know, or quarter-know what they are talking about, cover up their deficiencies by saying the sorts of things they think others expect them to say.

The advent of mass tertiary education has added to the confusion by making diplomas and degrees (never particularly reliable indicators of knowledge or skill) available to just about everyone. It is an environment tailor-made for spin-doctors, self-promoters and con-artists. The truly knowledgable, who may sound diffident, or even worse, by making unconventional or unexpected comments, struggle to survive. How do you know if your smooth talking financial adviser understands the first thing about tax? Or whether the young guy with the running shoes who tinkers with your office computer actually knows more than you do about what makes them work (if, that is, you can get someone from technical services to show up at all)?

Everyone is selling something. We know this. The difficult part is to distinguish exactly what it is. Advertisements for running shoes are indistinguishable from those for coffee beans. The maxim used to be 'don't sell the steak, sell the sizzle'. Now the sizzle does not get a look in (let alone the steak) – the advertisers want to sell us a kind of undifferentiated excitement invoked by the appropriate brand name.

Our susceptibility is enhanced by our terror at being thought out-of-date, inflexible. At one stage in my career I interviewed dozens of people in small business for a series of booklets I was asked to write. They belonged in two groups. The first group did everything out of the till and put the more misleading bits of paper they could find in a cardboard box which they gave to their accountant at the end of the financial year. The second group had a computer system in the garage or out the back which they had been persuaded to buy by a smart salesperson but which they had no real use for. Meanwhile, their books were being quite adequately kept, manually, by a middle-aged lady of stern appearance. But there was a lingering suspicion that books that could be kept manually could not be all that important.

The internet is a multiplicity of computers which are able to talk to each other through some very clever technology. But it has its limitations. People with useful information are not, on the whole, very keen on giving it away, unless they hope it may lead us to buy something from them, or to think better of them. (This used to be called advertising, before advertising was itself devoured by the world of blah – see above.) Therefore, finding useful information on the internet for nothing is like looking for a lounge suite on a rubbish dump. You might be lucky, but you have to sift through an enormous amount of garbage first.

When you come to think about it, the degree to which we venerate the means of communicating with each other is quite extraordinary. When George Bernard Shaw was asked what he liked best about living in the twentieth century, he replied 'modern dentistry'. Yet we don't talk much about dentistry, unless our teeth start playing up. Dentistry is boring, necessary and, in competent hands, works most of the time. Information technology is, at least superficially, more interesting (all those internally capitalised words must mean something). But because its necessity must be constantly talked up, or manufactured, we never hear the end of it. On top of that, computer systems of any complexity constantly come up with new and unexpected ways of not working. Most of us spend half of our time doing our jobs, and the remainder wrestling with the technology.

As Marshall McLuhan pointed out, communications technologies enlarge scale and scope, but not content. Thus the internet is rapidly being colonised by electronic spruikers, jostling for space and time with moribund websites and stale bulletin boards. Sometimes people talk to others with interests or problems similar to their own. What will they think of next? Pen friends?

The possibilities of choice must be relentlessly emphasised, while the possibility of choosing not to choose – of saying no – must be ruthlessly extinguished. Because silence is the great enemy of blah, we must have muzak in lifts and shopping centres, ghetto blasters on picnics, radios on bus journeys. The distractions have become the message.

All fields of human endeavour (except possibly nuclear physics) are vulnerable to blah. But management seems particularly vulnerable, perhaps because it is so much easier to talk about it than to do it. At a job interview recently I was asked to give my 'vision' for the department. It used to be that visions were religious apparitions which appeared to the poor and illiterate and could, with any luck, be used to bring in the tourists. Now people who run organisations, and even those who simply work in them, are expected to have them.

As the department concerned had more problems of a basic nature than you could poke a stick at, the question was more ridiculous than it usually is. I should have said so, but puncturing the bubble of blah that surrounds the average job interview ('we'll ask silly questions, you give us the right sort of silly answers, and we'll appoint the person we feel most comfortable with anyway') did not seem like a good idea at the time. So I tried to point out that a vision, to be workable, had to be generated by the people in the department. I myself thought that the department had some promise in a particular area, which I then proceeded to describe.

I recounted this to a friend, who was aghast. 'No, no, no!' she cried. 'You're meant to say you'll be the best such-and-such in the so-and-so.'

'But what if that's ridiculous?'

'Then say you'll be the second-best.'

Needless to say, I didn't get the job. I seem to remember that in times past, committees used to at least pretend to be interested in your ability to do the job, but all that kind of stuff has evidently fallen by the wayside. It is interview blah they are after.

I know of one organisation, struggling to hold its position in the marketplace, which was very big on the vision thing. Everyone in the company learned to talk about the vision, but unfortunately no one ever did anything about it. The vision became a sort of magic charm, like a fluorescent skeleton dangling from the rear-vision mirror of an early model car, expected to ward off harm. Finally, the vision was mugged by reality, and the firm went under. Another firm, under the influence of its vision, pruned off everything that didn't belong to the 'core business'. Too late, it was discovered that it was the non-core activities that had been subsidising the rest.

Where people feel compelled to conform to some external model of their organisation, rather than building up their own picture of it, they will use words for symbolic purposes, rather than as a means of communication. As a result, whole organisations begin to talk in blah. They fall in love with the language of change, forgetting that change can never be an end in itself.

The realities of most organisations are fairly simple – at a minimum, it is necessary to sell enough of your product or service to cover the costs of producing it. This is a fairly uncompromising imperative which the world of blah attempts, at all costs, to obscure. Take the fashion for customer service. All organisations are to some degree a conspiracy against their customers. The really bad ones are a conspiracy against those who work in them as well. Customer service managers are not there to make sure customers are happy, because that would cost the organisation a fortune. They are there to make customers sufficiently happy not to want to go elsewhere.

Sometimes even that desideratum gets lost in translation. One fast food chain I know of told its staff they had to improve customer service. When translated from management-speak, this meant they had to sell a certain number of dollars worth of meals each shift or they were out. The result was that employees practically assaulted each other in their eagerness to get to the customers first. Terrified rather than impressed, the customers took their business elsewhere.

Blah is to the cliché as a kit home is to do-it-yourself. Instead of a phrase being substituted, a whole framework of thought is there, ready for use. Take this typical brochure from conference-land. 'With global competition a growing challenge, the need for can-do attitudes is a common thread around the world.' If this means that it is better to have people who are positive about finding solutions to problems rather than those who are not, the statement is unexceptionable.

But life is rarely that simple. A person with a 'can-do' attitude is often planning to get somebody else to do the work. And not everyone with a 'can't-do' response should be jettisoned forthwith. They may simply be reflecting the reality that they do not themselves have the power to do what the boss wants, or perhaps the idea was not a good one in the first place. Blah merchants may appear to be strong on ideas, but they become evasive when asked questions. They see little point in thinking through the thousands of tiresome details that must be dealt with in order to get anything done. That is fair enough. But they sneer at the people who, being lumbered with these jobs, actually carry them out.

Antony Jay (one of the writers of the celebrated *Yes Minister* TV series) wrote in his book *Management and Machiavelli* of yogis and commissars – thinkers and doers. Some of the very greatest people have been both. Shakespeare was both a playwright of genius, and a practical man of the theatre who organised productions and managed a company. Trotsky wrote theory and led armies. Most of us, including most managers, are neither yogis nor commissars. Occasionally, we have good ideas, and occasionally, something that we organise turns out roughly as we anticipated.

It was for us that the word 'strategic' was invented. One of the truly great blah words, strategic means everything, and nothing. The term was invented by military commanders, most of whom had no idea what it meant either. Under its mesmeric power, organisations devoted themselves to the strategic management of everything they could think of, until it became clear that strategy was a way of denying reality, rather than engaging with it. When hamfisted personnel departments began to call themselves 'strategic people managers' it was clear something had to be done.

It was at this point that the consultants decided it was time for leadership to make a comeback. The idea of leadership is much more useful than the reality. In business as in everything else, much of the work that has to be done is just plain boring. Leadership suggests possibilities that are energising, colourful and dramatic. But leader-obsessed organisations magnify the idiosyncrasies of those in power, or paradoxically, they weaken themselves by giving too much power to kingmakers.

When they are unhappy about what is happening in their organisation, people will complain of a lack of leadership. In fact leadership is rarely a problem in management. Organisational life is designed to further the aspirations of the overly confident. The difficulty lies in getting good leadership, which means someone who understands the technicalities of the business while being able to hold their knife and fork properly.

Where confusion can be sold, we can be sure the blah-merchants will be there. The trick is to make everyone feel unsettled and insecure. One excellent way of doing this is to sell them on the idea that everything is changing, but without being too specific about the details. Organisations have often changed the things they do, and how they do them. In primitive times (that is, before we became obsessed with change), this was no big deal. If you explained to people what the new sorts of jobs were, they generally got the hang of them, and went about doing them. If they jacked up, it was usually because they felt they weren't being paid enough.

The secret has been to convince managers and employees that it is they who must change – they cannot fit into the new world without having a completely new approach to life. For an astronomical fee, 'change agents' will descend upon your organisation. They will ignore those aspects that probably do need changing (like unsafe working conditions or poorly trained managers) but they can be guaranteed to turn the place upside down with re-structurings and meetings. They will then depart, leaving behind them an admonition that change must be never-ending and that everyone must communicate about it constantly.

For the consultant, recommending more communication (provided one is vague about who with, for what, and when) is a pretty safe bet. Indeed, it is almost expected. No organisation, it is implied, can ever spend too much time talking about itself and talking to itself. (The fact that internal networks are clogged with useless messages that conceal those of real import is never discussed.) Managers usually interpret this sort of injunction to mean that they must issue more bulletins and circulars, exhorting this, prohibiting that, explaining something else.

Most organisations ruthlessly restrict communication upwards. This is because learning what actually needs to be done to make the organisation work properly confronts the manager with the effects of past sins of omission and commission. Middle managers, who have one ear tuned to the workplace and the other to top management, were able to pass some of this information upwards. But as middle managers have been eliminated, and those who remain have become more inclined to curry favour with their superiors, senior managers are less and less likely to learn what is happening.

I have seen organisations where the big boss makes regular visits to the troops, listening to comments and questions, even taking notes. It is an endearing spectacle, but unless the organisation is a very exceptional one, no one is going to use this sort of occasion to say what they really think.

The organisational retreat, much beloved of the conference industry, is another case in point. I have known grown men (and women) to weep when told they must attend another of these occasions. They are usually held, for purposes of corporate credibility and economy, in motels in faded or out-of-season resorts, in rooms with overly cold air-conditioning and no windows. Presentations are given, each one more deadly than the last. If the troops are unlucky, a facilitator of some kind has been called in to bring about some ill-specified kind of group bonding. Differences of opinion are not encouraged.

One manager I know of decided to keep the employees really up to scratch by convening a weekly meeting at which there was just one item on the agenda – the gross margin on sales. As hardly anyone understood what this meant, or how it connected with their own jobs, they gave up coming to the meetings. It was like the little boy who gave his mother a football for Christmas – he could see the point of it, but she needed to be convinced.

I have never known an organisation in which people did not want to communicate with each other, but the real killer of communication is mistrust. It is the political in all organisations that makes people hedge their bets, plan their next move, watch their backs. Small businesses are straight out dictatorships, large ones are generally oligarchies. Organisations tell us what it must have been like to live in a Renaissance principality. And they're the good ones. The bad ones tell us what it must have been like to live in the old Soviet Union.

Organisations are founded upon suppressed communication. Indeed, that is the modus operandi of the office. In harsher times, people who did not fit in got pushed out. The production line, the work gang, the hospital ward, the common room enforced a kind of solidarity. With its corridors and little rooms, the office invokes conspiracy, and separateness. It is a cool propinquity, based on the reception, processing and transmission of information. The same primeval instincts operate, but they must do so in more subtle, dissociated ways.

In contrast to production lines, offices allow people to move around fairly freely. There are files to be moved back and forth, visits to be made, meetings to be attended. Rumours flourish in offices because people have so many opportunities to exchange gossip, much of which turns out to be depressingly accurate. Most people instinctively trust the whispered conversation by the watercooler, particularly when official communications are sanitised to the point of parody, or simply record unpalatable decisions. And when we are being 'consulted' we know for sure we are being fooled.

Can anything be done about the world of blah? Perhaps not directly, but we could start by valuing a bit more highly its obvious antidotes—silence, reflection and clarity. In some quarters, to describe a document as 'well-written' is very faint praise indeed. Yet there is nothing more difficult than to be fair, interesting and precise all at once. Hardly anyone accomplishes it. Complex ideas cannot always be expressed simply, but they can usually, with sufficient skill, be expressed clearly. Clotted syntax and vague portentousness are too easily confused with profundity.

Blah is garrulous, without being articulate. As Australians, we do not value articulateness as much as we should. For me, the most shocking aspect of the regular inquiries into Australian police forces is not that so many officers are corrupt (the present state of drugs policy makes this state of affairs virtually inevitable), but that the language they use when talking to one another is so impoverished. It takes practice to talk well, a certain spirit and facility and a willingness to run playfully with an idea. Good conversation can survive packaged entertainment, but it cannot withstand that self-protective defensiveness, that refusal to be drawn, that characterises so many Australians. Perhaps we should let ourselves go a bit more. I don't mean the relentless chutzpah of American sitcoms, or even the choreographed emotion of the Australian cricket team taking a wicket, because that, too, is a form of blah. We should be encouraging not the assertive self-promoters with thick hides, but people who can tell stories, who notice things on the way to the bus, who are sensitive to nuance, and those who like, quietly, just to listen.

THE CULT OF MANAGEMENT AND THE DECLINE OF THE TEA LADY

Management is the great cult of our age. Conference halls resound to the mantra of its name. Consultants purport to sell us management expertise. Business schools profess to teach us how to practise it.

The problem is, no one quite knows what management is. The basic functional skills of budgetary control, financial decision-making, marketing and personnel management are all fairly clearly defined. But no one knows the magic ingredients which make one firm a success and another, apparently similar, a failure. If they did, they would presumably not be telling.

This has not stopped a seemingly endless succession of gurus of all kinds – millionaire entrepreneurs, resonant academics, consultants with charts – from promoting the latest management fad to eager audiences. Any organisation seeking to follow these various forms of guidance would have had a confusing time of it. It would have been successively down-sized, flattened, shamrocked, strategically planned, diversified, concentrated, re-engineered and, in all probability, bankrupted.

I imagine that successful managers adopt only those aspects of the latest fashion which suit their needs. Indeed, a senior bureaucrat in a large Commonwealth department once told me that the best response was to appear to be doing the latest thing, while getting on with running the organisation according to one's own sense of its needs. 'If we took every report seriously,' he said, 'we could not implement one change before the next one rolled along. The result would be chaos.'

To a significant degree, the cult of management is the creation of the management consulting industry. Old messages do not attract new clients, so the lives of successful entrepreneurs must be regularly trawled for new themes, much as religious orders might once have investigated the lives of the saints for useful hints on holiness.

A consultant, it is said, is a person who offers to tell you the time, borrows your watch and then forgets to return it. This is probably a little unfair – most consultants would give back the watch – but it is clearly in the interests of the consulting industry to talk up the idea that good management comprises a set of practices or principles which can be applied as readily in a baked bean factory as in a research and development laboratory.

The same principle is held to apply within the public sector – the formation of the Senior Executive Services of state and federal governments in the 1980s was based on the idea that a separate management group could be identified. The theory was that the successful SES officer in Social Security was exercising the same skills as one in Defence, and that managers could readily be transferred from one department to another.

It is ironic, given that so much thinking about public management is derived from real or imagined practice in the private sector, that successful senior managers in the private sector, tend to have detailed knowledge of the industries they lead, usually derived from long experience in them. Michael Eisner, the man who restored Disney's fortunes, knows a lot about making films. Bill Gates knows a lot about software. Rupert Murdoch understands the newspaper business. But that kind of knowledge cannot readily be traded by third parties, which means that it tends to be undervalued in the marketplace of ideas.

Skills may be transferable, but what they are for is not. This is not to deny that the idea of management has a useful core. It would never have survived this long if it had not. People have been building and running organisations for thousands of years – it took management to apply analysis to accepted practice. Frederick Taylor, the original time and motion man, showed how he could improve the efficiency of coal-shovellers at the Bethlehem steel works by a factor of four simply by analysing what the men did and improving the way they did it.

From this beginning, a rational paradigm of management has been constructed which forms the basis of most teaching and thinking on the subject. Rational management is premised on the belief that it is possible to analyse a situation and to make decisions which, however constrained by factors beyond the decision-maker's control, will produce an optimal outcome. Rationally derived solutions are implemented through collectivities of human beings, each related to the other by hierarchy or complementary responsibility. Managers are encouraged to think that setting objectives and encouraging people to work towards them, or penalising them if they do not, is the way to get things done.

As anyone will tell you who has worked in an unmanaged or poorly-managed environment, such thinking goes a long way. The problem is, we have assumed away the most difficult and interesting parts of management in order to render the concept portable, teachable and saleable.

It is difficult to discuss organisational politics without undermining, or appearing to undermine, the instrumentalist view of organisation from which the idea of management derives. Organisations are negotiated entities involving many interests, much as the state itself is the product of many interests. Machiavelli's Prince would have been right at home in the modern corporation. This resemblance between the mini-state of the organisation and the nation-state has been noticed by a number of writers. But it is not an easy perspective to reconcile with the ideals of rational management, which assumes an uncomplicated autocracy headed by a Platonic ruler of unimpeachable wisdom. The manager may have been restyled in more recent times as team-leader, coach and counsellor, but the rational paradigm dare not go further than that, lest it founder on the dreadful reefs of relativism.

The fact is, however, that management is impossible without power and dangerous without judgment. Bosses are more likely to damage company interests through want of judgment rather than want of technique. Yet we undervalue judgment and overvalue technique because judgment is difficult to measure and itself the product of perception.

A large part of the problem arises from the disjunction which has occurred between management (construed as scientific principles applied to organising) and organisation theory (the analysis of the structure and modus operandi of actual organisations). We know that real-life organisations are far from being the elegant control systems assumed by so many strategic management textbooks. They are arenas in which people compete for power and influence. Managers are caught up in this struggle as much as those they supervise.

When organisations are stable or growing, this internal competition need not be too damaging. But when competition outside intensifies, or the environment grows more uncertain, the power contours become much more obvious. When 'downsizing' occurs it is more like a game of musical chairs than a rational process. Those who are slower, older or less well-connected lose out. For their part, those with the most power will rarely question their own usefulness to the enterprise.

There are many examples of the consequences of this form of managerial solipsism. Consider the unheralded but certainly non-trivial case of the tea lady.

When I first joined the Australian Public Service in the mid-1970s, life without the tea lady would have been unimaginable. The tea ladies knew everyone and were either invariably cheerful or invariably doleful. As they tended to come from European countries with no tea-drinking tradition, their tea was often terrible. But that was part of the ritual, too.

The tea ladies began to disappear in the early 1980s, victims of a vaguely defined climate of financial stringency which nevertheless required its sacrificial victims. By any reasonable measure, the tea ladies were an asset to the organisations they served. Their salaries were low, and the service they performed of some significance. But the first law of cost-cutting is to target those who are most vulnerable, not those whose jobs ought to be eliminated. The tea ladies, as casual staff, were easy to get rid of.

The consequences of their going, while not trivial, were completely outside the understanding of the male managerial mind. The tea ladies washed and dried all the cups and took great pride in the cleanliness of the kitchen. Now public servants waste time making individual cups of coffee and tea in those same kitchens, which have long since degenerated into squalid communal messes. Above the overflowing sink someone has invariably sticky-taped a handwritten sign exhorting users to wash their cups. Few people do, of course, until the person with the lowest tolerance for unwashed cups (usually a woman) steps in and cleans up.

Both in the making of the tea and in the cleaning up, the

tea lady represented (to use the jargon term) significant economies of scale, all now sacrificed in the name of economy. The other losses are more nebulous, but no less important. The ritual of morning and afternoon tea held people together in patterns of civilised sociability. Now the chat time around the tea-urn (which was, contrary to rumour, fairly strictly delimited) has gone. People drink their tea or coffee at their desk, spilling stuff on files, leaving ring marks on the furniture. But human beings crave sociability, so they 'visit' each other, on some pretext or another, creating endless opportunities for annoying interruptions.

As far as I am aware, there was no central policy decision to get rid of the tea ladies. Rather they just faded away, as departments searched for easy ways of making savings. In one or two places – more enlightened or maybe more sheltered than the rest – tea ladies linger on, the last remnants of their species. When they are gone, no one will replace them. Organisational extinction is forever, too.

In the messy world of the organisation, power is never absolute. What happens may be initiated by those in the top jobs, but the way management controls are actually exercised depends upon relative power. If sacrifices are to be made, the more powerful make sure it is the less powerful who make them.

So hospital administrators get rid of nurses; school administrators get rid of teachers; university administrators get rid of untenured academics, senior public servants get rid of junior public servants, and junior public servants get rid of tea ladies.

In the private sector, because there is less ballast in the system, the effects of 'downsizing' can be even more abrupt. Anyone remember middle management? They were the people in bureaucratic organisations who ferried information up, and orders, suitably modified so that they were workable, down. In firms which produced goods and services, these were the people who saw that production targets were met, who fussed over the books, who knew at least something about what the line parts of the organisation were doing.

Middle management's mistake was that it not only became unfashionable, it was directly in the firing line. Middle managers don't normally belong to unions, so they were easier to get rid of than the unionised workforce. They were paid more than workers, so they saved the company a lot when they were removed. And it is top management, not middle management, which makes the decisions about who goes and who stays.

There is no obvious answer to this problem. Democratising decision-making (even if you could agree on how to do it) might induce total paralysis. Organisations cannot afford chummy incrementalism (maybe states can't either). But at the very least, the cult of the manager should acknowledge the qualified nature of the rationality it professes. It should also acknowledge the importance of personal qualities, as well as technical skills, in underpinning rationality.

Logically, if we wish to retain the advantages of hierarchy and minimise its disadvantages, we will want to recruit and retain people who are not only skilful but who have the character and judgment needed to exercise power wisely. Unfortunately, as Bertrand Russell observed, those who obtain power are usually those who want it the most, rather than those able to make the best use of it. If management is to be power in the service of rationality, rather than the other way around, we must confront the fact that managers are not the philosopher-kings of Plato's republic. They are products of the system used to appoint, train, evaluate and promote them.

A good system is one which judges people accurately. Managers who are shrewd judges of capacity and character will make good appointments. But they must also be able to appoint people who are themselves good judges. Ability to develop the abilities of others should, therefore, be the most highly sought-after characteristic of a good manager.

It follows from this that those who are best qualified to judge managers' abilities are those they supervise. Unfortunately, those who work for would-be promotees are rarely if ever consulted as to their bosses' suitability for promotion. It is always those in the next rank up whose opinions are sought. But these people may have their own reasons for supporting a particular candidate, reasons which have little to do with his or her suitability. (Of course, the underlings may have their own agenda, too. Overly glowing references may be as much as sign of danger as critical ones. We have all known people who 'got on' simply because they were able to impress people whose judgment was poor, and who were found out when it was too late. Shakespeare knew all about it when he wrote *King Lear*. Cordelia, the most-loyal daughter could not produce the right words to order. The scheming Goneril and Regan had no problem flattering the old boy into giving up his power to them. Managers, too, must understand seeming and reality, and the importance of knowing the difference.)

Management gurus discuss 'ethics' as though it were a sort of prophylactic against bad behaviour. Yet most people have a fair idea as to what they should do in particular situations where moral judgments are called for. The problem is, as religious writers have known from time immemorial, that implementing moral judgments requires moral courage.

Becoming a boss is, in fact, a considerable test of character. You must have self-belief while still being able to admit to mistakes. You must be tough, or your less scrupulous employees will run all over you. You must be flexible but also fair. You must be able to take a decision when one is required and stick to it. You must be able to trust other people enough to delegate to them.

It is difficult to teach people personal qualities and impossible to turn them into a module or a formula to sell to a company which has lost its way. But it is possible to impart some sense of their importance. In doing so, it will be necessary to ditch many of the bland case-studies of the management text-books and substitute something meatier. What about Stendahl's novel *The Red and the Black* as a study of ambition and its effects? Or *Hamlet* as a study of personality and decision-making? I would suggest that management trainees would be better advised reading and reflecting upon great literature than endlessly discussing the latest buzz words from conference-ville.

Finally, we need to be a little clearer about what management, as a useful rational enterprise, can actually do for an organisation. Peter Drucker, the man who invented management consulting, has made the most extraordinary claims for management as the 'active principle' of business, in essence, the basis of all competitiveness. Good management is the eyes and ears of business. But it cannot be its heart or its soul. No amount of good management can save a business in the wrong place at the wrong time with the wrong product. Nor can it save a business which has lost its self-belief.

I remember in one of the towns since bypassed by the Hume Highway between Canberra and Sydney, there was a cosy cafe where we stopped occasionally to have a meal. It was a little out of the way, but the chips were cooked just right, there was a friendly atmosphere, the place was spotless. An elderly Greek couple ran the business. Mum did the cooking, Dad took the orders and waited at table. On busy nights they had a middle-aged lady – red-haired, crisply dressed and with a friendly manner – to help out.

Some years later and after the town had been bypassed, we called in again for what proved to be the last time. The smell of the place had changed. There was a staleness where once there had been an aroma of food cooking. The floor was unswept. The toilet out the back had obviously not been cleaned. Even the rubber plant growing over the door seemed to have lost heart. The Greek woman was still there, cooking the chips, but the light had gone out of her eyes. Her husband sat stonily and watched the television. There were few customers. The locals had gone elsewhere, too.

The owners had clearly given up. They were on a downward spiral to another empty shop in another country town. Perhaps they should have seen the writing on the wall, sold out, moved on. But it is hope and heart which makes even those judgments possible.

Maybe new owners will buy the little cafe and have it running sweetly again. There will always be room for a good eating-place. But if they succeed, it will not be because they are better managers than the tired Greek couple. It will be because they believe in the business, and in themselves.

Management is a valuable concept precisely because it applies rational principles to collective undertakings. But rationality without power is ineffectual. And power without judgment is destructive. The concept of management can only be enriched by humanising it. If that means encouraging managers to cut back on the conferences, courses and consultancies and engage in a little self-conscious reflection, then so be it.

HOW TO GET ON

In one of Canberra's more up-market suburbs, there is an array of enormous houses stuck, rather incongruously, to a bare, west-facing hillside. They are all impressive dwellings, each perched atop a four-car garage and sporting some architectural accretion to indicate the prosperity of the owner – a tower here, a portico there. These are houses with little time or room for gardens. The hulking masonry butts right up against the fence.

As you look up the hillside, each house looms larger than the last until, at the very top, there is an absolute whopper overlooking the tiny backyards of all the others.

There is probably a view, of sorts, from the top. But the general outlook is far from prepossessing. Directly in front of these dream houses is a very down-to-earth stormwater canal, on the other side of which is a busy arterial road.

Before I became attuned to the importance of Getting On, I wondered why people with such obvious wealth would choose such an exposed situation, in full view of thousands of passing cars. Then the penny dropped. These were not houses to be lived in, at least, not primarily. They were houses to be admired and, if possible, envied. 'Look at me!' they shrieked. 'I've made it.'

The realisation that one has not made it, and is not likely to, can be one of life's sadder events.

I recall a friend who went to a school reunion. He had been to a Catholic boys' school, so it was not an occasion for the faint-hearted. Going to reunions, in any case, is best undertaken soon after leaving school when no one has done (or undone) anything, or alternatively left until those still standing can congratulate each other on their longevity. But my friend went during the dangerous middle years when old boys compare how successful they are, and old girls pretend not to recognise each other – well, not immediately, anyway. 'You haven't really kicked on, have you?' said someone at the dinner. The remark, cruelly intended, stayed with him for years afterwards.

My friend had a steady job, a nice wife, two beautiful kids. He was scarcely on skid row. But he had not made a million dollars, or become a professor, or been made a partner in a law firm. I would not describe him as a man of thrusting ambition. Like many of us, he had coveted the glittering prizes without actively pursuing them. But he still had an image of himself, somewhere, as a person of unrealised potential. To be reminded that he had fallen behind was to realise, finally, that the situation was probably irretrievable.

Considering its importance to many of the planet's most ambitious people, there is little reliable information about the process of getting on. As with all the really interesting things in life, academics have either not researched it or those who did so failed to get on as a result. No one knows if top executives are just like you and me, only more powerful, or whether they are quite different from you and me, as well as being more powerful.

Newsagents and bookstores are full of advice. There is a prevailing flavour of earnestness. One must set goals, establish priorities, and never waste time. One must win friends and influence people. But those who have got on *would* say that, wouldn't they? I suspect that just as with people's sex lives, the full story about how advancement is achieved is rarely told.

I have a theory that 'how to' manuals fulfil much the same function as recipe books. We like to flip through cookery books and imagine the wonderful dishes we might produce and eat. But we have no intention of actually expending the time and effort required. To do so would spoil the illusion that it is only lack of inclination that separates us from the realms of cordon bleu.

The same is true of books which purport to tell us how to be successful. Their invariably simple formulae arouse strong but vague feelings of determination and purpose. In fact, beneficial results are possible by having the book nearby, fully intending to read it, but never getting around to it. I have a friend who regularly takes *The Seven Habits of Highly Effective People* to the beach each year, leaves it face-down beside her as she sunbathes, and feels much the better for it.

Acting on the advice contained in these manuals can produce alarming results. A colleague who read *The One Minute Manager* became known as 'the White Rabbit' as he dashed frantically from one garbled appointment to the next, constantly afraid that he was running late. An acquaintance who went on an efficiency and effectiveness course took to advising workmates and friends how much time he was prepared to allocate to the conversation. The result was that people stopped talking to him.

Our attitudes towards getting on are deeply ambivalent. We like to think that those who have made it are figures worthy of our admiration. On the other hand, if getting on were an inevitable reward for virtue and hard work, why have we ourselves not succeeded?

We Australians like our heroes to be 'nice' – simple, unaffected and unassuming. We are disappointed, but secretly pleased, when journalists probing the lives of the rich and famous uncover disaffected friends, parents deposited in nursing homes, pets left unfed.

It is a matter of common observation that those who get on best in life are often not those with the nicest natures. Indeed, the qualities society says it values most (courtesy, honesty, loyalty) are not those it usually rewards. People who get on notice this hypocrisy early on. As Groucho Marx said, the two most important things in life are honesty and integrity. 'If you can fake those, you've got it made.'

Getting on requires the capacity to discern and to act upon one's own self-interest. This is not as common a talent as one might imagine. Most of us have a fairly short-term conception of our self-interest and are often too inhibited to pursue it, anyway. We are easily distracted. We get off the bus to look at the flowers or are captivated by a piece of music. We are not homo economicus.

Clearly, it is not necessary to be particularly bright, at least in the academic sense, to be successful. Tycoons don't have to do well at school. Even among the well-educated, the most intelligent are, on the whole, the least successful. Research tracking the careers of Harvard Business School graduates found that there was no correlation between intelligence and achievement as measured by earnings. It seemed to boil down to that exciting but somehow disturbing quality – ambition. Ambition simultaneously suggests that good things may be claimed by aspiration, rather than by worth, and that the world is manipulable.

I remember once talking to a group of students from developing countries about strategic thinking in organisations. One of them took me to task. 'Our problem is not a lack of strategic thinking,' he said. 'We have plenty of people who are strategic thinkers. But they have just one strategy, and that is to advance themselves.'

Getting on means taking a totally instrumental view of the world, doing only what will feed ambition, determining the opportunity cost of each chance encounter. Few weigh up every chance encounter, meticulously, to determine whether this is indeed superior to the next best option. But some people do. You can pick them out at parties, looking over your shoulder, sizing up the next prospect.

In politics, in business, in academe, it is those who are most ruthlessly single-minded who achieve prominence. The meek may inherit the earth, but they do not normally get promoted. Even those who are merely realistic about their abilities are no match for the brashly confident. This no doubt explains why so many 'top people' are so very bad at their jobs. The skills needed to get to the top have little to do with the skills actually needed to exercise power well.

This mismatch occurs throughout organisations, of course. It is just that the effects of incompetence tend to get worse as you go higher, because the skills required are greater, and it is easier to cover up mistakes. The work of a bad cook or a bad cleaner is apparent to all. A poor chief executive takes longer to flush out.

The qualities required to get on are determined by the qualities of those who have already succeeded, in an infinite regress. In a famous piece, C. Northcote Parkinson (still one of the most acute commentators on corporate life), described how it was possible for organisations to self-destruct because their processes for determining who was to 'get on' had become completely subverted by idiots.

In the days when company directors were chosen on the basis of their social contacts and their ability to eat lunch, it was scarcely surprising that so many companies suffered from poor governance. As the corporate collapses of the 1980s gathered momentum, the vacuous nature of many of these worthies became apparent. It is astonishing how many of them understood little or nothing of the documents put before them to sign. Too often, those who did understand them had insufficient courage to stand against the tide. Now that selection is made on the basis of social networks alone, and lunch is no longer the institution it was, we may hope for some improvement.

Unfortunately, the social networks are not what they were. Barely had the older-style boys' clubs recovered from the depredations of the corporate cowboys, than they were being transformed by those mysterious and magical beings, the entrepreneurs. What, you may ask, is an entrepreneur? Well, Brad Cooper is (or was) an entrepreneur.

We learned quite a bit about Brad from the Royal Commission into Australia's most dramatic corporate collapse, that of the insurance company HIH. Brad, by his own admission, was not too sharp on the details of running a company, but my goodness, could he get money out of people! Here's how he did it. He simply badgered them until they gave him what he wanted. He managed to get $100 million out of Rodney Adler to prop up his business selling home security systems, a feat which so surprised Rodney, he had to sell his own company to HIH in order to get over it. As HIH in turn went down the gurgler, a 'river of money' flowed in Brad's direction. In the witness box, an HIH financial executive recalled the 'incessant battering' he received, as the young entrepreneur rang him at least ten times a day, every day.

As the HIH story unfolded, everyone wondered what had happened to corporate ethics. Sometime in the mid-1990s, the corporate world had discovered the existence of ethics. Codes of behaviour were constructed for other people to follow, but unfortunately the go-getters continued much as before. It is not that unethical behaviour necessarily takes you to the top. It is just that too exacting a sense of right and wrong creates such difficulties for the meticulous person that he or she never makes it.

Take the apparently simple matter of paying bills. Fortunes have been founded on the principle of paying one's creditors only under threat of court action while sending large and persistent persons to the premises of one's own debtors. In such a system, nice firms run by nice people go under.

It is not true that power corrupts. Most of the work has been done on the way up. TV shows that depict a world of goodies and baddies in which the goodies always win are popular precisely because they are so unrealistic. Most people (the people who do not 'get on') would like to think the world is like that, although they know in their hearts it is not.

Those who get on know the value of such convenient fictions. If too many people turn into cynics, life becomes unworkable. The right balance is a moral code practised, however intermittently, by about 90 per cent of the population. Of those who do not practise the moral code, five per cent (the poor and stupid) can be put in gaol, thereby satisfying the prejudices of the majority. The other five per cent can get on with running the show.

The rest of us have our work cut out keeping track of them, let alone controlling them. It is true that the law catches up with some of them, but that tends to happen only when the mess is politically visible. The truth is that it is hard work holding people accountable, and few of us have the stomach for it.

Social conventions are not much help in this respect. The institutions of childhood – family and school – are designed to break people in, to socialise them. It is where girls learn to be nice and boys to be obedient. It is where most people acquire the rituals of concern for others, and learn to care about what others think of them.

Parents and teachers are in the business of making

judgments, many of which will be faulty or biased. Those with the confidence to Get On know this instinctively, and are fairly resistant to the opinions of others. The world is a wider and more various place than the schoolyard or the family.

But you must be able to spot the opportunities. The world's richest man, a Hong Kong Chinese called Mr Lim, found that he could make money by buying property and selling it for more than he paid for it. He reasoned that if he did this many times over, he would become very wealthy. He was right.

So much for the entrepreneurs. What about the professions? Here the going is both tougher, and easier. While everyone no doubt benefits from training, only the untalented really need it. The world is full of intelligent-enough people who can absorb the fundamentals of the law, or medicine or engineering. They make money out of it because society gives them a framework within which to do so. But because there are so many people with these forms of knowledge, getting on means competing against other, similarly qualified people, within a large organisation.

Getting on in big bureaucratic organisations means sniffing the breeze, and sussing the lie of the land. It means sorting out the jobs which will confer easy credit from those which are likely to be tougher. It means having a nose for power. Above all, it means winning and retaining the good opinion of others.

There are three main ways to do this. The first is to plough on, assuming that virtue will be rewarded. The second is to network like blazes, so that everyone who matters knows who you are, even if no one is too sure what you do. The third is to hitch your wagon to an older colleague who will appropriate your work, but will also bring you some reward.

Those who follow the first course are usually men. They are intensely 'focused', which means they ignore anything and everything not directly related to their immediate self-interest. They work hard, fifty, sixty hours a week and more. For women, this course of action is always more difficult to pursue, not because women are intrinsically any less 'focused', but because it is more difficult for women to rebuff the demands and expectations of others.

Women still, by and large, value affection and good relations more than men do. The son of a well-known earth scientist told me that his main memory of his childhood was of a locked study door behind which his father worked. He was forbidden to interrupt him. His father was available only at the times he decreed, and they were never enough. The bitterness was very plain. I do not know of many women who would see professional advancement as so important that they would deliberately forfeit a relationship with their child to achieve it.

The networking alternative requires less concentration. But it does require a certain rat cunning to know who to network with, and also a certain ruthlessness to ignore those who are unlikely to be of use to you. Ready-made networks are a decided advantage. The ultimate in ready-made networks is aristocracy, which at least had the advantage that birth determined whether you were in or out. In democracies, parents must go to inordinate lengths (such as learning to play golf) in order to create networks for their children.

The third possible strategy for those climbing the organisational ladder is to find a patron. This method is faster than networking, but can be higher risk. To locate your patron, you must find a reasonably prominent person in your organisation or line of work, and flatter him or her outrageously. You would think that eminent persons would be able to detect these transparent strategies, but such is the vanity of human nature they very rarely do. Finding the right patron is a bit like assessing the field in a horse race. The higher in the organisation your patron is, the less risk you run that you have backed a dud. The returns will be less than if you pick someone lower down whose rise you can share in. But in that case, you run a risk that you will hitch your wagon to someone who is going to fail, or fall from favour.

There are other traps for the unwary in this method. If genuinely talented, it is likely that you will in fact know more than your prospective patron. If he or she is secure in themselves, this will not matter, and may in fact commend you to them. If, however, your patron has Got On for other reasons, you have a problem.

You must be better than average, but no so much so that the patron fears being eclipsed. Indeed this 'just enough' principle is very important. Some people have an ability to attract support from others precisely because they have cultivated the art of being non-threatening.

Successful people understand intuitively that they must always reinforce the self-importance of those with power. They know that things are rarely decided objectively or, still less, fairly. It is all to do with seeming. As Elizabeth observed in *Pride and Prejudice*, Mr d'Arcy had all the goodness and Mr Wickham all the appearance of it. Most people find it difficult to make objective judgments based on the evidence before them. Or, to put it another way, no matter what the evidence, they will reach their conclusions on emotional grounds.

I have observed this on selection committees. People will make judgments about applicants' attitudes and motivations on the slenderest evidence. Once, when interviewing people for a publishing position, one of the applicants revealed that he had a home office. Others on the committee immediately assumed that the applicant wanted to use the job as a backstop while he set himself up in a consultancy business.

Witness, too, the case of a middle manager made redundant after 30 years in a bank. He applied for jobs a little below the rank he had once held, hoping to maximise his chances of re-employment. But employers rejected him because they thought that he was simply trying to take it easy. (Is that what they themselves would have done in the same circumstances?) He applied for more senior jobs and was successful.

I have left until last the business of getting on in the creative and intellectual worlds. In some ways, this is the most political task of all, because everything depends upon reputation. If you write romances or thrillers, or pop music, your reputation depends upon your sales, which in turn depend upon your ability to entertain.

If you aspire to what Harold Bloom calls more 'difficult pleasures' – if you want to be an artist of some kind – matters are more complex. The world produces far more people who want to be artists than it does people who are genuinely interested in art. Even among this group, relatively few can make up their own minds about what is good and what is not. The rest, who think that art must somehow be good for them, have no independent powers of judgment at all. They are much more interested in writers than in what they have written; painters than in what they have painted.

To reach these people, you must attract the attention of those who write personal profiles for the newspapers or who line up people for interviews on radio or TV. A publicist, I am told, works wonders because he or she knows how to fit you up with a 'hook' to get people interested.

Whatever the field, though, you must get cracking. As Jack Lang is supposed to have told the aspirant Paul Keating: 'You are a young man and when you get to Canberra they will all tell you that you have plenty of time. But the truth is you haven't a second to lose.' Keating hit the ground running, and was an ex-PM by the time he was in his early fifties. Although the sheer numbers of baby boomers will soon make it quite chic to be just a little bit – you know – old, only the young and the driven have the combination of ignorance, energy and belief in the system necessary for getting on.

What about those of us for whom it is already too late? In the words of Bob Dylan, we know that 'there's no success like failure, and failure's no success at all'. I suggest that we console ourselves with genealogy, which is a form of retro-spective getting on. With a little effort, everyone can find ancestors who were notorious, famous or rich. If that does not appeal, there are always Past Lives. I have never met anyone who was a washerwoman or a vagrant in their Past Life: everyone was a pharaonic priest at least. Moreover, you don't need to bother with all that messy archival research. There's always an American to teach you how to do it. Pricey, but they have to get on too, you know.

TAKE ME TO YOUR LEADER

When the fuss about management seems to be dying down, everyone suddenly starts talking about leadership. Good leaders are paragons – a mixture of Bill Gates and Albert Einstein with a touch of the Dalai Lama thrown in. Hardly anyone measures up, of course, so there are now courses to teach you how to do it. There are two schools of thought about leadership training, if you don't count the one that says leaders are born, not made. The first has it that people learn about leadership by being thrown into fear-inducing situations such as whitewater rafting or caving. Apparently companies pay large sums of money to have their employees subjected to these experiences. The theory is that participants feel so good about surviving, they conclude that the workplace is not so bad, after all.

The second approach is more theoretical or, at least, more abstract. Participants who have little or no opportunity ever to exercise leadership reflect upon the leadership style they might adopt if given the chance. Then they undergo some personality tests. Adults like personality tests for the same reasons kids like playing in sand pits. It's absorbing, you don't have to think about it too much and you're not committed to the final result if you don't like it.

It is generally agreed that leadership is about getting things done. With so many reports, strategic plans, guidelines and other exhortatory documents lying around, actually achieving things seems not a bad idea. On the other hand, effective leadership may mean that silly ideas get implemented faster than they otherwise would. When the inventors of organisational re-engineering discovered that it did not work in 70 per cent of the organisations in which it had been tried they, rather ominously, attributed the failure to a lack of leadership.

Undoubtedly, one of the best aspects of leadership is when it changes. How satisfying it can be, watching from the relative safety of the lower decks, to see previous favourites rolled, and new ones installed. But life doesn't necessarily improve as a result. In these troubled times, it is difficult to predict which particular group of carpetbaggers may fall upon your organisation. No matter how poor the outlook, it is as well to remember that things can always get worse.

It is much easier to pick bad leaders than good ones. 'His men would follow him anywhere,' wrote one commanding officer of one of his subordinates, 'but I suspect it would largely be out of curiosity.' Similarly, the absence of good leadership is easier to detect than its presence. Weak leaders are unable to control the endless baronial politicking that characterises all organisations of any size, but in an era which is understandably squeamish about these matters, we are reluctant to confront the relationship between effective leadership and power. The historical evidence is not all that encouraging. The English kings and queens of the Middle Ages had real power, but most had no idea what to do with it. Some kings could cut the mustard, others were clearly not up to the job. Henry VI was far too pious to survive. William II managed to quarrel with both barons and Church when just one would have been sufficient. Richard II started out well, but was no match for his wily cousin Bolingbroke.

Successful monarchs, like Henry VII and his granddaughter

Elizabeth, understood two things – violence and money. These two commodities were important because the medieval nobility was a giant protection racket. If you did not pay up, you were slaughtered and your goods confiscated. It was, in a way, the ultimate privatised society. Having a good spin doctor was as important then as it is now. Richard III probably committed no more murders than the average monarch of the period and died nobly on the battlefield, but Shakespeare put a spin on his activities, and even his appearance, from which his reputation has never recovered.

I note that the American Business Wisdom literature, currently my very favourite category of reading for long journeys, steers clear of giving contemporary business persons as examples, because you never know when they, or their companies, are going to go broke. Praising a dud is embarrassing enough, but if the former high-flyers have also been bending the law and have been found out, they are paraded around in handcuffs (the Americans not being inclined to mess around in these matters) – a corporate look which tends to linger in the mind of even the least attentive business student. Dead business leaders are less risky, but as most of them grew rich through cornering the market in something or other, or preying on the poor and weak (sometimes simultaneously) they lack the inspiring qualities which are currently in favour.

Political leaders offer a more promising field because the worst about them is generally known or suspected while they are alive, although even here, there have been some problematic cases. The verdict on John F. Kennedy, for example, was skewed for some time by the tragedy of his assassination. The heroics of the Cuban missile crisis were counterbalanced by Kennedy's role in embroiling the US in Vietnam, and by a decidedly murky personal life and connections.

Military leaders seem safer, and few American writers can

go past Robert E. Lee and Ulysses Grant, both equally revered, even though Lee was technically a Loser. Perhaps it doesn't matter so much if the Loser is also an American. George Washington and Dwight Eisenhower succeeded both as military leaders and politicians. Interestingly, both had unassuming qualities about them. Washington did not go as far as the Roman general Cincinnatus and return to his plough once his military duties were over, but he did refuse the crown offered him by the army. Napoleon, who had the supreme bad taste to crown himself, was too full of hubris to last long.

I am not sure who the Australian equivalents of these leaders would be, although Paul Keating certainly had a touch of the Napoleonic about him. We have little taste for the heroic, and find it difficult to believe that any of us could achieve greatness in anything, except possibly sport. Our historical style has been to admire people who got on with the job and did not make too much fuss about it. Ben Chifley, a modest man, remains most people's favourite political leader (more resilient than Curtin, less cocky than Hawke, and homelier than Menzies).

It is said of Chifley that on one occasion he took a woman's meat order over the phone rather than tell her that she had accidentally got onto the prime minister instead of to her butcher. In this age when no one is ever contactable by telephone at the first attempt (unless you actually wanted to leave them a message), the thought of the prime minister answering the phone 'live' is almost too surreal to contemplate.

Business and industrial leaders are a little more tricky. Most Australians assume that anyone who has made any money has done it illegally or, at the very least, by evading tax. If this was ever an overstatement the Howard government and the Democrats have made it a reality by changing everything about the tax system except the top personal income tax rate. In these circumstances, I suspect that bypassing the taxman will become more of a national obsession than ever. I don't know if Alan Bond ever paid any tax, but as he apparently stole most of his money from unsuspecting investors to begin with, the question is fairly academic. But at least he copped it sweet, and went to gaol, unlike the egregious Skase, who mocked us through his oxygen mask from Majorca.

Among the media barons, property developers and horse trainers who appear in the rich lists there are few figures who inspire. Although his methods were unorthodox and his ending abrupt, I would think Ned Kelly remains our best-known private sector leader.

I am not sure why Ned continues to interest us so much because, as a bushranger, he was far less successful than Frank Gardiner, known as 'the organiser of outlaws', who was the mastermind behind the Eugowra Rocks gold robbery in the central west of New South Wales, and managed to die in exile, after being pardoned by Sir Henry Parkes. Still, per-formance indicators for bushrangers are a little difficult. I am still puzzling about my current favourite, Thunderbolt, an operator so subtle at least some of his victims insisted that he had not robbed them at all, but had simply asked them for money which, of their own free will, they had decided to give him.

Even where success is unequivocal (like winning the Nobel prize, or making a great deal of money before one is forty), there is not much to be reliably learned from it, because studying success is an example of that supreme methodological sin, selecting on the dependent variable. While we think we may understand the attributes of suc-cessful leadership (making decisions in a certain way, winning the confidence of subordinates) we cannot be sure that unsuccessful leaders do not show the same characteristics.

Ernest Shackleton eschewed the privilege of the gentleman leader, and saw that his men, rather than their officers, received the warm fur sleeping bags on the dreadful night the *Endurance* sank beneath the Antarctic pack ice. On the long journey in the ship's lifeboat to South Georgia, Shackleton's spirit remained indomitable. Yet Shackleton had no idea what he was doing, and it was the skill of the navigator, Worsley, who saved the expedition from disappearing in the wild seas of the South Atlantic. Indomitable spirit and a democratic style may be helpful to survival, but they are hardly sufficient.

We know that in some circumstances, leadership is not a luxury, but a necessity. There is simply not time to caucus about sailing a ship and no one has found an effective way of running an army without some kind of hierarchy. Elementary communications theory shows that it is always more efficient to route communication through one central person than from one person to another. Divided authority rarely works, as the example of the two quarrelling explorers, Hume and Hovell, reminds us. At one stage near Tumbarumba relations between the two got so bad that Hovell, the British officer, insisted on continuing south through the mountains while Hume, the native-born bushman, wanted to take a more westerly route. They agreed to go their separate ways but, according to the convicts who accompanied them, fought over a frying pan and were about to divide the expedition's tent in two, before Hume said Hovell could have it.

Our ideas about leadership, like our ideas about organisations in general, are based on metaphors. We think leaders ought to be able to lead because we imagine organisations are pyramids, with the leader at the top. We imagine that those 'on top' have more power than those 'on the bottom'. If A directs B and B directs C, then A, by definition, directs both B and C. In fact, the organisational logic of the firm will have been created long ago, and it will assign a role to the chief executive rather than empower him or her. This explains, in part, why re-organisations are so enduringly popular. They enable new power spaces to be created.

As practising manager David Mitchell noted: 'Organisations tend to be hierarchical because it is traditional for humans to organise themselves that way and to go where the leader points. A hierarchy satisfies tribal instincts.' To some degree, all humans are hard-wired for hierarchy. We like to think there is someone in charge, someone who knows what's what, someone who will tell us what to do. In short, we like to have a Boss. Our longing for causal certainty tells us that the boss will surely save us. On the other hand, we suspect that the boss knows no more than we do.

Whether the boss represents some atavistic need to be led, or is simply a convenient fiction for focusing blame, is a moot point. Like most people, I am not averse to being led, provided the leader makes decisions that I approve of. When the leader makes decisions of which I do not approve, he or she is clearly a bad leader.

Most people in an organisation are convinced that they could run it better than the existing management. For those ostensibly at the top of an organisation, the sensation is not one of being 'in charge' but rather of being at the mercy of the organisation. The boss is a lightning conductor for every dissatisfaction.

I once asked someone in charge of a large company which depended upon large-scale contract work what is was like being a leader. 'Leader!' he snorted. 'I'm just the chief bloody salesman. If I don't bring in the orders, we don't eat.'

I asked a small businessperson the same question. 'We have to make payroll every week,' she said. 'It concentrates the mind.'

A colleague was equally definite. 'A leader is someone

who keeps the shit away from you so that you can get on with your job.'

Every organisation tells us where its most important people reside. They have panelled offices, deeper carpets, private car parking spaces, secretaries. But the most important person is not necessarily the real boss. Everyone knows who 'the real boss' is, because he or she supplies the organisation with its imagination, its stories, its rumours. The real boss sets the emotional and ethical tone. When Paul Keating said it was time for Hawke to go 'because he has stopped nurturing us', we knew exactly what he meant.

To call the top manager a leader is, however, a complete misnomer. Small organisations don't really need to be led, and large ones cannot be, at least, not by one person. It is simply not possible to project leadership that far. Various techniques can be used to magnify the role of the leader, as giant screens are used at rock concerts in stadiums, or massive banners at political rallies. But unless fear is the sub-text, all this is something of an illusion.

If it were true that chief executives controlled organisations, we would expect that their activities would reflect that function. In fact, when we look at what chief executives do, their activities bear little relationship to the planning, directing or controlling activities so beloved of the text book. They are either out selling, or putting out fires, or dealing with paperwork, or talking to people.

The boss has responsibility for more important decisions than those 'lower down' and, usually, has access to more information. We reason from this that the person 'at the top' also has the best view of the organisation. We forget that picturing an organisation is an exercise in virtual reality. What if the organisation is not a mountain like Mont Blanc (that is, a mountain sticking up out of a plain or highland) but a mountain like those of the Blue Mountains west of

Sydney, with the bulk of the employees on the plain at the top, and the chief executive in the valley below? An inverted pyramid has just as much validity as the classic one. It suggests that information flows downhill, rather than up, and that the chief executive may in fact have far less knowledge than the sum of the organisation's employees.

We think because we can draw a hierarchy, we must have created one. But what if the organisation is an orange, with the boss secreted away in the middle, surrounded by self-contained segments? What if the organisation is a cube, with vertices each occupied by a person controlling that plane and no other? What if the organisation is an ant-heap, a honeycomb, or a tangle of spaghetti?

Organisations are like those famous Picasso pictures where the parts are viewed from many different angles at once. We cannot see them 'whole', because even the simplest and smallest organisation deals with many things of which it is not completely aware. Take your own family, for example. Can you describe why and how it survives, and what its key relationships are with the 'not family' world? Systems thinking probably comes closest to the type of thinking required, but we cannot hold 'in our mind's eye' a conception of the flows and relationships involved.

When I am teaching people about organisations, I encourage them to draw a picture of their own organisation, as they see it. The results are amazing. Many people cannot get a grip on their organisation without drawing some kind of hierarchy. Others draw the way the organisation actually works, showing the power clique that makes most of the decisions, the flows of favours and resources and the ramifying thickets of dead wood.

Most people will draw much larger those parts of the organisation which actually affect them. Some feel as if they are working in isolation, others that they are engaging in constant flack avoidance. One person drew himself behind a wall, while sales and marketing engaged in range warfare on the other side.

Everyone sees organisations differently, because the physical and psychic realities are so different. We can see the buildings the firm operates in. We see people moving about. We see people sitting at computers, talking on phones, holding meetings, making cups of coffee. The annual report tells us some other details: how large the entity is, what it does with its money (roughly). The key factors however, will always be the intangibles, otherwise everyone (or no one) would make money on the stock exchange.

Let us consider the information generated by organisations. There is no way an executive can deal with all of it, or with even a small part of it. Each layer of management filters the information out, as it should. The amount of information reaching the chief executive is no greater than that received by the first supervisor. But it relates to the whole organisation.

Very few people have an incentive to tell the chief executive the truth. If they have stuffed up, they must find ways to cover over their mistake. Compulsive honesty finds no favour in the corporate or political worlds. George Washington may have been unable to tell his father a lie, but he would have learned to lie as President.

It used to be the case that bosses worked their way up through the organisation. When they reached the top, they probably forgot what it was like on the sales floor or the machine shop, but at least they had been there. In the 1990s, many senior people seemed, by some strange form of miscegenation, never to have been anywhere near the functional parts of any organisation. They moved, with their entourages, from one highflying role to the next, collecting packages, golden handshakes and Cabcharge vouchers along the way, but without ever having accomplished anything.

Most organisations survive on the common sense of the people working in them. In the late twentieth century, however, so remote have leaders and their entourages become, that they inflict upon employees something called 'change management'. As in the Middle Ages, those at the top have no understanding of what those at the bottom actually contribute. Huizinga, the great historian of the period, reports that chroniclers of the nobility were almost completely ignorant of the role of those who actually did the work of medieval society – the artisans, peasants and merchants.

I would argue that if an organisation does not function well at its lowest levels, it must fail. What do people 'down the bottom' see? They see the customers. For a large organisation with many customers (such as a chain of department stores) each person employed as a sales assistant sees only a small proportion of the total group. Between them, however, they have seen every customer over the past year.

Yet the information they possess is rarely collected by management. 'We could sell ten times more of these,' said the saleslady when there was no more stock of my size, 'but we have to take what the manufacturers send.' On another occasion, in a department store, I asked for a popular children's book. It turned out that they had it in stock, but it was not on display. 'If it was up to me, I'd have it out the front, but we have to display the books the buyers tell us to,' said the sales assistant apologetically.

When outsourcing first came along, it seemed a godsend. People up and down the land looked forward to seeing the last of purchasing departments so slow and inefficient it was easier to bend the rules rather than use them; information technology support services which hoarded manuals and took ages to respond to requests for help; accounts departments which produced expenditure figures so unreliable and out of date that everyone kept their own records; public relations departments which could teach the secret service a thing or two; maintenance people who made *Waiting for Godot* look like an action movie. Alas, by some malign principle, it was nearly always the good guys who got outsourced, forced into draconian contracts by a resurgent purchasing department.

In these strange times, many organisations, particularly in the public sector, combine gung-ho adventurism with the most soul-destroying timidity, when no one will take a simple decision and be responsible for it. In this environment, intelligence shines like a good deed in a naughty world. So I honour the lady on the counter who described to me how she always asked extra questions of the people she saw, to make sure they had the form they needed, not the one they thought they wanted. And the occupational health and safety inspector who said she was more interested in getting firms to have a system that worked, rather than one which conformed to every element of the law. And the sexual harassment officer who 'had a word' to offenders before the whole ghastly bureaucratic system was invoked that so often grinds common sense and ordinary judgment into dust. And to anyone who, through desperation, luck or flair, manages to keep problems lawyer-free. That, to me, is real leadership.

LETTER FROM ACADEMIA

It's now eighteen months since, rather late in the day, I left the public service to become an academic. The transition has proved more difficult than I anticipated. Like all those, I suspect, who have never taught for a living, I underestimated the sheer physical demands of standing up in front of a lecture room full of people, and attempting to inspire in them an interest in subjects which, while dear to me, are as esoteric as Sanskrit to most of them. I'm told that the first twelve months are the hardest (and yes, I know about the holidays).

Academic life is very different from life in the bureaucracy. It is grittier, somehow, closer to the sweat and to the appetite of everyday life. It is also noticeably less well accommodated. The toilet paper is thinner, the offices smaller and horrors! you have to go through the switch to make an interstate call. Most people use emails, which you can send anywhere, anytime, although whether they are read or not – or having been read, are replied to – is another matter.

The students, once one gets used to how unaccountably young they are, are on the threshold of decisions which will shape their lives. You hope that what you have to say to them will prove, if not memorable, then at least useful. Like an actor, or an entertainer, you notice that your audience varies from performance to performance. Your energy is either absorbed by them, leaving you drained and somewhat bewildered, or it bounces back, refreshing everyone.

Academic life is unrelentingly political, because universities are pressure cookers of personality and ambition. Once past their earlier, peripatetic years, people stay for decades in the one institution where they must compete against their colleagues in annual promotions rounds. As with any profession, the incentives you face are shaped by the system which determines how and whether you advance. In the bureaucracy, it is proficiency at tasks determined by institutional or polit ical necessity which attracts the favourable notice of mentors or patrons.

For academics, the maxim has always been 'publish or perish'. Promotion supposedly came to those who published regularly in obscure journals. It didn't matter whether anyone actually read the papers or not. It was sufficient that they were there. But having witnessed numbers of cases where people both published and perished, I am now not so sure. I have heard of academics getting jobs because they could play cricket or make up a bridge party. Selection committees are so large and so unwieldy, and the time taken to assemble them so inordinate, it is not really surprising that it is the candidate who everyone remembers, rather than the one with the best qualifications, who tends to get the job.

Being an academic is, in fact, three jobs rolled into one – administrator, researcher and teacher. Each academic must find a balance between the three which suits them, and each must work out ways of developing and showcasing their particular talents. Recognition depends not just on performance, but on skill in self-promotion – much the same as any job, you might think, except that academia, despite its trappings of collegiality, is more individualistic than most.

In the bureaucracy, it is the job which defines the person. In academia, it is you, plus the reflected prestige of your

institution, which must impress. You will need to create a reputation or, at the very least, a persona, if you are to succeed.
You might affect a cap, a bow tie or dye your hair green.
Men can always go for interesting elbow patches on their
jackets, or wear socks with their sandals.

Having established your image, you must have a clear sense
of your own priorities, so that you choose to do only those
things which are likely to bring you favourable notice. You
must figure out ways of getting out of activities, such as
administration and teaching, which do not impress promotions committees. And you must network tirelessly because
you will need mates as much as any apparatchik in the New
South Wales Labor Party.

Reputation-building is an art in itself. In the physical and
biological sciences, the discipline of scientific method, however politicised, gives at least some measure of objectivity to
the creation and sustenance of reputations. In the social
sciences and humanities, where there is no single accepted
paradigm governing inquiry, the making of reputation is a far
more individual matter. There is ample room for heartache,
envy and skulduggery, all within the confines of institutions
which, more than most, constitute worlds unto themselves.
This is, no doubt, why the cloisters of ancient universities and
the windswept walkways of new ones provide the mise en
scene for so many novels.

Universities have it all. There are the students, who are
trying to learn and to grow up at the same time, many of them
(at least if excuses for handing in essays late are any guide) in
circumstances of hair-raising difficulty. Then there are the old
lags, encrusted like barnacles on the carcase of the institution,
full of strange theories and prone to sudden outbursts. There
are colourful characters, like Malcolm Bradbury's History
Man, always with an eye both to current fashion and to the
main chance. There are big daddies, den mothers and drifters.

There is endless gossip, much of it unnervingly accurate, about who is 'in' for which job.

Everyone gossips in every organisation in the country, of course. But in academia there is an additional relish to it, because the process of preferment is so unpredictable. In fact, I have come to the conclusion that it is pretty well random. Different selection criteria are applied at different times, for different jobs, in different institutions. The newer universities, including the former colleges of advanced education, at least strive for a form of bureaucratic fairness, although more, one suspects, because the administrative staff are relatively more powerful in these institutions than because of any innate commitment to fair play.

The further one ascends the hierarchy, the more arbitrary the process of selection becomes. Very senior appointments, such as that of vice-chancellor, are in a class of their own. While applicants from other backgrounds have, on occasion, succeeded, the vice-chancellorship of the University of Melbourne, for example, is, according to tradition, filled by a member of the engineering, medical or legal professions. At the Australian National University, the coveted position alternates between the physical and social sciences. Much depends upon whose 'turn' it is.

In past years, at least in the more traditional universities, no woman need apply either. That unspoken prohibition has gone, but it is still the case that women find it more difficult to get promoted in academia than they do in the public service. I have yet to see any convincing explanation as to why this should be so, other than the fact that there is more discrimination against women in academia than in other parts of the public sector.

It seems a most extraordinary irony that feminist academics who earn their living exposing the sexist attitudes and practices of society at large, do so from within institutions where sexism, like a miasma, is all-pervasive. I do not mean that it is overt, or even obvious, simply that in a profession where opinion determines just about everything, there is little that women can do to overcome prejudice. Women may be accepted as lawyers, doctors and business executives because they produce results as good as, if not better than, the men. In academia, especially in the tweed-jacketed Australo-British variant we have inherited, it is especially difficult for women to crack the code.

While there are many male academics who unreservedly accept women as equals, there are some (and not necessarily the older ones, either) who believe, deep within, that women are not really quite up to it when it comes to the higher forms of cerebral activity. There are men like this everywhere, of course, and most women know within sixty seconds of commencing a conversation when they are dealing with one. But there are also women academics who harbour secret doubts, if not about themselves then certainly about their female colleagues, and who, whether consciously or not, pay more attention to a view when a man utters it, than when a woman does.

I think it was the economist and policy adviser Helen Hughes who pointed out how variable was the quality of Australian academics. There are good and bad departments in the one university, and good and bad people in the one department. Despite the centralisation of the Unified National System, conditions vary a lot, too. There are universities with the latest in teaching technologies and others where they can barely rustle up an overhead projector. There are universities with munificent facilities for staff and others where you have a pie and chips in a noisy refectory with the students.

But all academics, wherever they are, are united by their fear of university administrators. Academics are worried that control of 'their' institutions will be wrested from them. To avert this fate, they have chosen to do a most curious thing. They load themselves up with the most routine and time-consuming forms of administration it is possible to devise. Doing this work, even doing it well, earns no kudos. It could just as easily be done by well-trained non-academic staff. But it is jealously guarded because to relinquish it would be to relinquish power. The fact that, despite these tasks, academics have singularly little power in universities seems to have escaped everyone's attention.

What of the future for the academic profession? Despite its individualism, the character and attractiveness of academia as a career depends upon the status of universities, their congeniality as workplaces, and the role which society calls upon them to play. Until the 1980s, when universities were places to which only a tiny proportion of school leavers went, academics were rare and somewhat remote beings who, by and large, society left alone to pursue their esoteric calling. Universities were havens for some notorious incompetents, but they were also sufficiently laid-back to allow odd-balls and obsessives the space to move and the freedom to develop their ideas.

When every post-school institution in the country calls itself a university (and the transformation of the colleges of TAFE cannot be far away), the very notion of a university is obviously on the verge of dissolution. If academics are not to become glorified high school teachers (although with far larger classes than any high school teacher would tolerate) it will be necessary for universities to re-cast themselves in a new mould, to professionalise their management, and to offer students far more clearly articulated and distinctive learning experiences than they do now. While doing this, universities will need to offer the conditions and the encouragement to attract the bright and creative minds they must have to prosper intellectually.

Can they make the necessary changes? One of the problems is that the contemporary university has been discovered by government or, to be more accurate, by politics. There are votes in providing university places for almost everyone who wants one, regardless of their ability and commitment and regardless, too, of society's real needs. We have management consultants and lawyers coming out of our ears, while finding a good bricklayer is a virtual impossibility. Governments appear to believe that there is political mileage in warehousing the young for a few years after they come out of school, rather than depositing them in an increasingly uncertain and volatile labour market. How else to explain the current lack of interest in mature-age students who, being older and more sure of what they want, perform significantly better at university than do school-leavers?

With government interest, comes government control. Having deregulated everything in sight, the federal government decided to centralise the direction of universities to a degree which would not have been out of place in the former Soviet Union. Allowing universities to offer more full fee-paying places has changed little. Australian universities must dance to the tune of the federal government, able to compete for the lucrative overseas dollar, but not so as to offer a better deal to Australian students.

For the controls to be loosened, the federal government and the universities would have to learn to trust each other. Unfortunately, given the vituperative and often brutal character of Australian public life, this seems highly unlikely. Most academics think of bureaucrats as faceless functionaries, while most bureaucrats think academics are both over-rated and perpetually on holiday. In some ways, there is more of a divide between the two types of public sector employee than there is between either and the private sector.

Meanwhile, academic life will continue, with its feuding,

its hard slog, its occasional bursts of inspiration. It's not a place for the go-getter, nor yet for the faint-hearted. The innovators are all in industry (at least, I hope they are) and the greedy have gone into the professions. As for me and, I suspect, others who are intrigued by it all, I'll hang in here a little longer. I'm working out how to teach public administration to the video generation. Now there's a challenge.

IT'S ACADEMIC

Back in the 1960s, when I was a teenager, we used to watch a TV quiz show called 'It's academic'. The contestants were teams of high school students, and the questions could be demanding. I remember my sisters and I loved to second-guess the answers from our living room.

Quiz shows based on knowledge have long since been replaced by contests which celebrate consumerism. But even if someone were to revive 'It's academic', the name would have to change. Whereas thirty years ago the connotations of 'academic' were something like 'intelligent', or even 'knowledgeably high-powered' now it is a synonym for futile or irrelevant. 'The scoreline is academic,' says the sports commentator when the result has ceased to matter.

Words change their vernacular meaning for many reasons, ignorance among them. But I don't think that is what has happened to 'academic'. Now that going to university has become commonplace, the ivory tower has lost much of its mystique. While science retains some respect in the popular imagination, the social sciences and humanities are seen as marginal activities, far removed from the realities of daily life, and preoccupied with problems which no sensible person would be concerned with.

In the midst of so much turmoil in universities, when

conscientious academics must juggle the multiple roles of teacher, researcher, administrator and marketer, it may be unfair to criticise the most sacred of academic activities, that of scholarly publishing. But it seems to me, as someone who has struggled with the conventions of academic publishing herself, that the hoi polloi may have a point.

When academics write books for the wider public, we do it as well as anyone. But when we write for each other, our prose is laboured and impersonal, our focus narrow and our purpose obscure. Check out any of the hundreds of journals in which social scientists seek to publish, and you will see what I mean.

Here is a world in which the 'real' world is hardly recognisable. It has been lost, beneath layers of bibliographic mulch, vague or overly-specialised jargon, and an all-encompassing desire not to say anything new or different. Even honest empirical research that addresses questions of practical relevance is presented in such a po-faced fashion as to rob it of vitality and immediacy.

Let me hasten to add I am not inveighing against the dreaded postmodernism here. Rather, I am arguing that, for a number of reasons, scholarly publishing in many fields and in many styles has fallen into the deadly trap of derivativeness and pedantry. The dark side of what it is to be an academic, the kind of stuffiness which made George Eliot's Mr Casubon such a spine-chilling character, threatens to overcome the forces of inquiry, originality and risk-taking.

Readers are irrelevant to this kind of writing. The publication of a paper is a performance indicator, a notch on the belt, another centimetre on the curriculum vitae. The sad reality is that most papers end up communicating with no one at all, not even other academics. They are simply not read. There are hundreds of journals in the social sciences and humanities. Even those academics who dutifully 'keep up with the literature' read only a small proportion of the papers published in their field. This is a viable strategy because many, perhaps the majority, of papers have very little to add to the existing body of knowledge: no interesting speculations to offer, not even errors productive of further thought. They have been published precisely because they are safe. If they had something to say, there might be a risk that the author had got something wrong. And editors of academic journals shrink from error as from the plague.

Most academics start out with high hopes and brave intentions. But they soon learn that it is better to be published than to be brave. So the thinness of the enterprise is disguised by as much scholarly apparatus as can conveniently be assembled. The conventions of academic publishing ensure that as much time as possible is expended in getting to the point, if indeed there is one. It is scarcely surprising that students resist reading such work, when most of the article is devoted to scholarly throat-clearing and the recitation of bibliographic pedigrees. The result is that five or even seven thousand words are used when one or at the most two thousand would have sufficed. Longwindedness is everywhere confused with profundity. Indeed many academic journals will not even consider work which is shorter than a prescribed minimum length. Surely a rethink of these conventions – for that is all they are – is long overdue.

It must be acknowledged that in the social sciences at least, there is not much to be said that has not been said, better and more plainly, before. And in fields such as history, where the terrain of what might be written about is limited by the availability of sources, there is a problem of diminishing returns. With less virgin territory and ever more people attempting to stake out their claim, it is scarcely surprising that each person is attempting to till a smaller and smaller patch of ground.

Sorting out who is worth attending to, and who is not, is, in part, a subjective business. The very nature of the social sciences and humanities means that knowledge is, to some degree, politically shaped. By this, I do not mean that what social scientists write is value-laden, although obviously it is, but also that what is accepted and what is not depends in a very direct way upon the power of professional cliques to impose their own paradigms. Social scientists are right to point out that sciences such as physics are not immune from this problem, but somewhat slow to admit, at least publicly, that their own disciplines are riddled with it.

For all their internal tumult, the sciences and mathematics adhere to generally accepted objective standards of assertion and verification. Radical ideas have a hard time being accepted. But to be taken seriously, an explanation must rest on repeatable experimental evidence or on theoretical proof which can be checked. Research builds on or refutes the work of others, it cannot quibble with it, gloss over it or ignore it.

In the social sciences, on the other hand, the absence of a consensual paradigm of inquiry means that what is considered acceptable depends as much upon who is doing the considering as it does on the characteristics of the work. A paper summarily rejected by the referees of one journal can be hailed by another. It is all in the approach.

If, as a characteristically frank American explained to me, you still can't get published, the remedy is simple – start your own journal. This, plus the fact that many academic journals are subsidised in various ways by the universities in which they are lodged and do not have to cover all their costs, no doubt accounts for the enormous proliferation of journals that has occurred in the last twenty years and continues even in the current, more austere, climate.

Subjects which are largely verbal in content (such as

political science, history and sociology) are not difficult to grasp in their fundamentals (although to say anything new requires great imagination and skill) and, provided one can find one's own plot of ground to till, and the time necessary to do the work, it is not too difficult to build up the intricate verbal tapestries favoured by journal editors.

In contrast to the sciences, where checking what people are doing is almost as important as making new advances, there is surprisingly little direct engagement between academics within the pages of a given journal. Compatibility of approach has already been assured (or the paper would never have been published) and in any case, what is there to check? If the paper simply re-works the observations of others, a different interpretation may be possible, but which version is to be preferred is a matter of taste rather than truth. Empirical work is, or should be, a different matter. But there is little to be gained by subjecting the methods or conclusions of others to rigorous critique.

When battle is joined with adversaries, feelings may rise very high indeed. But for the most part, academic life in the intellectual sense is not based on argument about the implications or significance of particular ideas, but rather consists of disputes arising from different ways of approaching similar problems. It is almost mandatory for an article or paper with any kind of synthetic intent to begin with the caveat that 'the field is not well-defined' or that 'basic terms are used in different ways by different writers', making any real progress in the subject virtually impossible.

Where there is no independent standard of proof, the decision to publish depends upon the opinions of anonymous referees, whose role is to uphold scholarly standards by relating the submitted work to prevailing norms. The idea is simple enough. If someone else has managed to get the idea published, it must have been quality-tested in some way. A

new idea, on the other hand, will not have much of an intellectual pedigree, so the temptation is always to side with the
known, rather than the unknown.

The problem is exacerbated when the development of
new ideas depends upon attracting the support of research-
funding committees. The funders want to know what they
are buying, which implies that the research has either already
been done, or is not of much interest anyway. Funders do not
want to take a punt on anything too risky, nor are they
happy about supporting relatively unknown people.

A friend of mine, a scientist, once pointed out to me how
competitive every branch of academic life – including
scientific research – had become. The people who succeeded
in this environment were very bright, she said, but she
wondered whether they had the capacity for independent
originality which characterised the true greats, at least some
of whom would never have qualified for further support on
the basis of their undergraduate record.

Imagine, for example, Charles Darwin applying for a grant
from the Australian Research Council. Only a modest
academic record. And he wants to travel? To collect things?
To test a theory he can hardly begin to specify? What is his
track record? What are his publications? What do his referees
say? Exit Charles Darwin. (In fact, it was Charles Darwin's
father who funded his research as naturalist on board the
Beagle. His equipment for the voyage cost £600, while the
Admiralty extracted £50 per annum for his board and
lodging.)

It takes a certain kind of personality to succeed in academic life. Sustained effort is required, robust self-belief, and
a capacity for finding the most efficient path to advancement.
There can be few careers in which success is more peer-
determined. In most professions, it is usual for peers to award
the glittering prizes, but there are normally other people to

impress as well – customers, clients, interested parties of various kinds. Barristers must win the occasional case; doctors cure the occasional patient; merchant bankers clinch the occasional deal. For academics, one must impress one's peers.

This is a process of exquisite balance. Peers are also competitors, and in a crowded field, there is more to be gained from withholding praise than bestowing it. Mentors are required to smooth the path, and to make the necessary links, but are often hard to find. As in other fields where networks yield resources, support and preferment, most women (and also many men) find it difficult to make much headway. Very few academics would discriminate actively against a colleague. But when it does happen, there is little redress.

One of the saddest but also, I think, one of the most truthful books I have read in a long time is Andrew Riemer's *Sandstone Gothic*. When a young man, Riemer was dissuaded by a self-seeking American academic from doing his PhD dissertation on a playwright whom he found interesting, ostensibly because someone else was working on the same topic. No study of the playwright ever appeared. Soon afterwards, as editor of a collection, this colleague rejected without proper explanation a major essay of Riemer's putting forward ideas which subsequently became important in the discipline. Years later, Riemer observed this same person centre stage at an international conference at which he himself was no more than a peripheral player. Riemer does not say his career would have been different had he done the work he wanted to do. But it might have been.

For Australian academics, there are additional problems. To what extent does one concentrate on Australian phenomena, and to what extent does one attempt to build an international reputation? For philosophers and to some degree for economists, the problems are not so acute, provided one sticks to theory. (This probably explains why those Australians with international reputations outside the sciences tend to be philosophers.)

In more empirical pursuits, choices must be made. Papers laboriously crafted from Australian experience cut little ice when submitted to overseas journals. 'The examples are all antipodean,' sniffed one English reviewer when I tried this stratagem. Americans can write about their domestic situation and it is international. When Australians do the same, it is parochial.

We should have a tradition of Australian thought which is like the flora of the Hawkesbury sandstone – spiky, vigorous, independent, original. But while the cringe may have departed from other areas, in academic life it lives on. It may even have got worse. The top Australian academic journals, craving respectability, are often stuffier than their overseas counterparts. The same sense of constriction applies to monograph publishing as well. Australian academics are not comfortable kicking around the big ideas from an Australian perspective. Reading Francis Fukuyama's *The End of History and the Last Man*, it seemed to me that a work of such breadth, power, and tendentiousness would be most unlikely to originate in Australia. That's partly because the market for this kind of writing is small, or is believed to be, and few publishers are prepared to take it on. But to bring Nietzsche into brilliant conjunction with a universal theory of history is not the sort of thing Australian academics do. Unlike the self-confident Americans, we encase great thinkers in too much reverential aspic to deal with them in this way. As for an Australian Foucault – it is only people overseas who get to pronounce upon the world without the aid of footnotes.

In some respects, indigenous thought may even be on the retreat. Intellectual innovations, like those in other fields, will usually be imported. But in the post-war years, perhaps because of Australia's greater isolation at that time, it seems to me that there was greater ingenuity in adapting the borrowings to Australian conditions. Since then, the borrowings have been equally uncritical on both the right and the left.

We imported public choice theory from the US, and used it to change policy without considering whether the analysis applied equally or in the same way to a parliamentary system based on majoritarian party rule as it did in the unashamedly spoils-based institutions of US democracy. Our native brand of political economy, which had understood Australia's place within a world economy dominated by great powers, survives only in small pockets, outflanked by conventional economics on the one hand and cultural studies on the other.

If we are ever to understand the complex politics reshaping our society, academics should be leading the charge. Yet misguided priorities are causing many academics to waste time in generally unproductive work. We laugh now at the medieval scholastics who spent years debating whether or not Jesus carried a purse. I wonder what future generations will make of their descendants' fascination with such concepts as 'performativity'. I am not arguing that academics should turn themselves into consultants, although there is nothing like a little consultancy work to demonstrate just how useless much academic theorising is in giving guidance for the solution of practical problems. I am saying that trained mindpower is in short supply, and that in the social sciences in particular there should be more emphasis on tackling what so-called ordinary people think are the real issues, such as why the salaries of business executives depart ever more obscenely from those of their employees; or why the billions of dollars spent on improving the lives of Aboriginal people seem to have failed to reach so many of them. If that means work that is a little rough around the edges, then so be it. To amend a once-popular adage, if a thing is worth doing, it is worth doing badly.

I have left to last the question of academics' working environment, the universities themselves. Have we created a system which will nurture the best people? I think that must be open to doubt. Over the past 40 years, we have built a vast web of institutions for credentialling the young to perform useful tasks in society. This is a necessary function, but one which sits poorly, on the whole, with the outlook and ambience needed to generate new knowledge.

Successive governments must be well-pleased with the way they have milked the academic labour market. They have extracted much higher levels of productivity, while paying salaries which have barely moved in real terms and have fallen well behind those available in the public service or in business. There is not enough money to pay the munificent redundancies which oiled the wheels of change in the public service. With few options to restructure, universities have ruthlessly exploited contract teaching labour. There are few organised programs of staff development, and sometimes startling inconsistencies when it comes to filling jobs.

The result is that, of the best people in any field, very few are likely to consider an academic career, or at least one built around the hard slog of teaching, administration and research – when you get the time for it. This has been the situation for some time in disciplines such as law and accounting where there is strong demand from business and the public service. But the attractions of life outside the university are beginning to affect career paths in the mainstream social sciences, with implications for both research and for teaching. Over time, a vicious circle sets in. As the calibre of working academics inexorably declines, it is more and more likely that the best students will be turned off further work. As a result, universities risk failing their most precious and fragile cargo – people with the capacity to think differently.

There is certainly something to be said for making a

university place available to all those who want it. Those who promoted this policy genuinely believed that the university experience was a good one, which would enrich the broader society as more people took advantage of it. Beyond a certain point, however, it is not the university which changes the punters, it is the punters who change the university.

Remember that education is what Fred Hirsch (in *The Social Limits to Growth*) called a positional good. Its value to any one person depends to some extent on others having less of it. As competition for jobs tightens, and more people want to go to university, the relative value of a particular credential declines. A doctoral student of mine confided that everyone at her level in her public service department had a master's degree, so she needed a PhD if she was going to get on.

If there were an infinite supply of talented people, this credentialism would be tolerable, if incredibly costly. But talent is in short supply. So standards, inevitably, fall. A run-of-the-mill bachelor's degree today is probably at much the same intellectual level as a good school leaving certificate of the 1970s.

The shape of the system we will end up with, regardless of the political party in power, has been discernible for some time. The better-endowed universities are beginning to carve out an elite position for themselves, while the rest will make do with various kinds of journeyman education – a bit like the system we had in the mid-1980s, really, only more expensive. It would be preferable if universities were to differentiate horizontally (that is specialise in different things) rather than vertically (doing the same things more or less well). This would also help academics to work more cooperatively together on larger, more socially relevant projects.

For the necessary rationalisation to occur, however, the federal government would have to start showing some genuine leadership, and encourage the concentrations it wants, rather than leaving the structure of the system to the forces of a very lop-sided form of competition. There would also need to be a change in the Australian public's belief that every course should be available to every student as close as possible to his or her home town. That, in turn, would require expenditure on campus accommodation and allowances for living away from home, so that students could attend the more specialised institution of their choice.

The management of most Australian universities needs much closer attention. While state and federal public services have undergone a largely unnecessary managerial revolution, universities, in a desperate bid to bring in more cash, pursue offshore (and sometimes onshore) business ventures they have neither the expertise nor the experience to run professionally. In most cases, the university has no idea whether the venture is making money or not, because the financial reporting and management accounting systems are simply not up to the task. The effects of these ventures on the true business of Australian universities (the education of Australian students) can only be guessed at. At best, our young people are being short-changed the time, attention and resources that are their right. At worst, they are being fobbed off with sub-standard degrees.

While the worst of these problems will no doubt sort themselves out, the underlying health of public tertiary education will not improve without more money. It is a curious state of affairs. By virtue of our deregulatory zeal, we have constructed (we are told) the best economy in the world, one that is amazingly resistant to the ills which beset the Europeans and even the Americans, and yet we are unable adequately to support its most important public activity – the education of the young (and not so young)

Whatever happens, the traditional culture of Australian

universities has gone for good, not entirely a state of affairs to be deprecated. Those inclined to romanticise the past should refer to Andrew Riemer's account of the Goldberg years at Sydney University. The details of the controversy have about as much interest to most readers as the Goulburn cathedral dispute of last century. But what it does reveal is the terrifying vulnerability of younger and junior staff in the days of the god-professor. Any organisation can turn toxic, but most will have at least some escape routes. Academics are trained for just one thing, and if no other university will have them, they are stuck.

What kind of management *is* appropriate for academics, however, has yet to be determined. It has always struck me as odd that performance agreements are widely used in the public service where they are difficult to administer fairly (because the work is mostly team-based) but arouse tremendous opposition in academia, where people work much more as individuals. Sooner or later, some form of performance management will become general in universities. It would be to everyone's advantage if academics were to start developing the necessary frameworks for themselves, rather than have them imposed by administrators with little understanding of the realities of contemporary academic life.

In the meantime, Australian universities in the early years of the twenty-first century are not exactly fun places, but some of us can still look on the bright side. A colleague was telling me how much he liked working at the University of Canberra. 'Why is that?' I asked. 'Well,' he replied, 'at the last place I was at, one half of the department had not spoken to the other half for more than thirty years. It was pitched ideological warfare the whole time. Whereas here,' and he broke into a broad grin, 'all your disputes are about money. It's so refreshing!'

Amen to that.

DISMANTLING
THE STATE

I have occasionally wondered what it must have been like for scholars of the Soviet Union when, almost overnight, they found their lifelong object of study had evaporated, its categories obsolete, its assumptions redundant. I am now beginning to find out. A transformation has occurred in the subject matter of Australian political science. The Australian state I thought I knew has been dismantled, and regardless of where subsequent politics may take it, the fundamental changes are irreversible. John Howard may dither over selling the remainder of Telstra; he complains that the labour market is not yet sufficiently flexible. But the key change is the first one – as the New Zealanders discovered when they confronted the effects of their own era of revolutionary change, re-involving government in areas it has vacated to new players, is virtually impossible. It is possible to put the brakes on, but to imagine a new direction, let alone take it, requires a stronger nerve than most governments can summon.

Australia's state governments have, without exception, abandoned the deregulatory zeal which characterised New South Wales and Victoria in the early and middle 1990s, opting for personable leadership and the familiar nostrums of economic growth and death to drug dealers. But the great state institutions of last century – the insurance agencies; the public transport bodies; the public health and education systems – have yet to find a form that will meet the needs of the twenty-first. Although the electorate dislikes and distrusts economic rationalism, no government has had the daring or the skill to transcend it.

Unlike the Soviet Union, the Australian state was not transformed because of popular disaffection, but because ruling elites decided that the traditional Australian way of doing things had to be abandoned. The new ideas made a formidable cocktail. To the deregulatory zeal of Australia's native economists was added the state minimalism and anti-unionism of Mrs Thatcher's Britain, with a touch of Kiwi executive violence thrown in for good measure.

The mantra of the economic rationalist – that competition cures all – became the ideology of the Australian federal government, regardless of the party in power. As politicians, John Howard and Paul Keating could not have been more different. But on matters of economic management, they were as one – if it moves, deregulate it. If it doesn't, sell it. If you can't tell what it is doing, contract it out.

The Hawke–Keating Labor governments and their supporters and apologists in the media entrenched deregulation of the economy as the major policy priority. Thus tariffs were reduced; telecommunications and banking deregulated; and in the states, water, electricity and railways restructured. Under the National Competition Policy, Commonwealth trade practices law has been extended to the states' business jurisdictions by the passage of complementary legislation.

The Howard government took this agenda still further by deregulating the labour market through the mechanism of workplace agreements. It sold what it could of remaining federal assets, ordered several outsourcing exercises (although at least one, involving outsourcing of information technology, was subsequently rescinded) and devolved many programs (although not funding for them) to the states. Only the need to negotiate legislative changes through the Senate, where minor parties continued to hold the balance of power, stopped it from going further, faster.

The intellectual rationale for these changes is clear. The discipline of economics has a powerful prescriptive stance built into it – the crystalline perfection of perfectly competitive markets. From this belief, it follows that the answer to any economic problem is to add more competition to the pot. If competition cannot readily be found, the next best thing is to manufacture it. Thus, government helped to set up Optus as a competitor to Telecom and created a new regulatory body to oversee the two carriers, and to determine the conditions under which the carriers could deal with their own customers. Ultimately, regulation of the large and unruly telecommunications market was handed to the Australian Competition and Consumer Commission, a more highly-powered successor to the Trade Practices Commission.

But the Australian market is not very big, and in industries of this type, there is a constant tendency towards monopoly. Bob Menzies created the famous two airlines policy to keep a semblance of competition while giving each operator (one public, the other private) a reasonable slice of the action. The new boys thought they could do better, but several decades, umpteen failed start-ups and one spectacular collapse later, we have only one nation-wide domestic operator, the ever-more-arrogant Qantas, now effectively foreign-owned.

Like most revolutions, this one will create new opportunities for those clever enough to seize them; but it will also do great damage to the social fabric which the old order sustained. The reformers, to do them justice, have not been unmindful of social equity. But they show few signs of understanding the magnitude of the changes they have set in train.

So far, an adroitly managed welfare state has absorbed

most of the casualties. The middle-aged men who lost their jobs when manufacturing was wound down in the 1970s and 1980s were tided over until they qualified for the pension. High youth unemployment, particularly among the unskilled, has been massaged away by labour market programs (that is, subsidies to employers to take them on). Public servants have had their way into retirement smoothed by handy redundancy packages.

They may have been the lucky ones. The axe is now beginning to cut deeper, and its swathe is wider. As financial conglomerates form and reform, employment in the banking industry will continue to fall. Public sector workforces will be slashed, further eroding the employment base in rural and regional Australia. Companies struggling to maintain profitability will be forced to lay off more workers.

One by one, the props which supported what Paul Kelly and others have called the Australian settlement, were kicked away. Industry protection has gone; the industrial relations system which ensured a place for unions within it is being dismantled; public enterprise in all its forms is being sold off if profitable, broken up into so-called business units and closed down if it is not; and the rest converted to user-pays.

The traditional edifice was the product of a compromise between business and labour; between city and country; between manufacturers and rural producers; between free trade and protection. Bring it down and you alter the balance of power in the community. Bring it down without the consent of those affected, and you risk unprecedented social division.

No one asked Australians about which, if any, aspects of their society they wanted changed. In a sense, the issues were too fundamental to be discussed at election time because political campaigns tend to dramatise what is happening at the time (such as economic boom or bust, or the arrival of boatloads of asylum seekers) rather than the big questions of politics or economics. In any case, the major parties were not offering much of a choice. Had they been asked, no doubt ordinary Australians would have found fault with the traditional institutions. Industry protection was too high and often undiscriminating; the unions could be bloody-minded and backward, and so were too many employers; Telecom and Australia Post, as well as other public services, were the butt of endless criticism.

I doubt, though, that there would be general approval of the remedies chosen – a zero-tariff policy with few compensating support mechanisms; an end to collective bargaining in industrial matters; sell-offs to one section of the community of assets previously owned by everyone; and endless 'downsizings' and restructurings of just about every public authority or government business enterprise in the land, with the exception of the Australian Institute of Sport.

Those promoting change are quick to tell us that there is no alternative. The world is beating down our defences, they say. We had to change our ways. I have never been entirely convinced by this kind of argument. It is too often put forward by those who know perfectly well that there are alternatives, but find them either inconvenient, costly (to them), or ideologically unpalatable.

Since the first decades after federation, the Australian way has been to use regulation of the private sector and investment by the state to achieve social goals. Thus the regulated financial system was used to make cheap money available for housing. Protection of manufacturing taxed consumers and exporting industries (mostly rural producers) in order to provide jobs for city-based people and for immigrants. Banks operating in a protected environment (because before deregulation, foreign-owned banks could not obtain licences) ran numerous rural branches which even in the 1960s and 1970s must have been uneconomic. Telecom favoured residential over business users. State-owned electricity utilities favoured some businesses over residential consumers. Water authorities delivered cheap water to irrigators. Subsidised rail authorities balanced subsidised road users.

These kinds of practices drive economists nuts, because the cross-subsidies are hidden, and because public enterprises tend to politicise what should be commercial transactions. But as a means of promoting social equity, they have much to commend them. Equity and efficiency are entwined through the system of production, rather than being seen as two separate concepts, one social and the other economic. Dismantling such a system in the name of economic efficiency inevitably leads to a reduction in social equity.

It is claimed that explicitly designated community service obligations, funded from the budget (such as requiring a bus company to operate uneconomic routes), are the way to continue subsidies if they are socially justified. But the managers of corporatised utilities will not argue for them, and governments will remove budget-based subsidies when they think they can get away with it. Those displaced from public employment or from regulated industries and who fail to find work are supposed to be compensated by the social security system. But social security does not make up for the loss of a job. If anything, as former Labor politician John Langmore and economist John Quiggin argue in *Work for All*, there should be more public investment rather than less, if we really want to do something about unemployment.

The economic benefits of deregulation are more hypothetical than real. Lowering costs to business, we are told, will lead to the creation of new jobs. As uncompetitive businesses fold, their place will be taken by those better able to use the community's resources. This may be so, but the economic models on which the predictions of massive efficiency gains are based merely *assume* that this will be the case. They do not demonstrate it.

The proponents of deregulation have been quick to claim that the excellent growth performance of the Australian economy since the mid-1990s is proof that their policies work. Yet when we look more closely, we see that growth has occurred, not in areas exposed to international competition, but in those parts of the economy that are shielded from it – in construction of homes and offices, and in services of various kinds.

Within specific industries, there have been pluses and minuses as a result of deregulation. Certainly, phone calls are cheaper, but in aviation we have ended up with one pre-eminent domestic carrier (Qantas), which now faces much less competition over the whole of its network than in the days of the much-maligned two airlines policy.

The official unemployment rate disguises huge levels of hidden unemployment – people who, compared to the bad old regulated days, will never work, or will never work again.

The proponents of change should demonstrate that the benefits outweigh the costs, but somehow the costs are never weighed in the balance. Competition, in particular, is a two-edged sword. Take the railways. A good deal of heavy freight used to be moved on railway lines which were not viable without a subsidy. With the breaking up of railway authorities, these lines were the first to be closed, and many were torn up. Putting more and bigger trucks on the roads is the inevitable consequence of what is happening in rail. One wonders how many accidents involving these juggernauts it will take before the average family motorist starts to understand the risks that are being assumed on his behalf.

Consider telecommunications. Telecom built and maintained a network which was a major public asset. Part of its profits were absorbed by too many staff. But the government, as the major shareholder, received significant dividends. The benefits of the old order have become the costs of the new. Optus, originally the competitor created by government to balance Telstra, invested billions of supposedly scarce capital in duplicating a network which was substantially already there. Instead of new services like cable television being efficiently provided through one underground network, subscribers in Sydney and Melbourne must be 'wired up' with kilometres of ugly and intrusive cable strung from street poles.

Blind Freddy knew that Telecom was a highly inefficient organisation. Its work practices had not kept up with changing technologies. Technicians finished their allocated tasks in a couple of hours and spent the rest of the day doing 'foreign orders'. But it was also a fairly effective organisation. In a country with one of the most thinly dispersed populations in the world, nearly everyone had a phone.

Given this situation, most people would say, find a way of fixing up Telecom. Strengthen its board; clarify the balance between its customer service, community and industry development obligations; and let management and workers get on with it. The concept of the government business enterprise, an extension of the older Australian idea of the statutory authority, was designed to achieve these objectives, and Telecom benefited from being so designated. But there had to be competition, so Optus was licensed as a second carrier to compete with Telecom/Telstra. It is a bit like discovering the family car is a bit slow, and then buying another one to make it go better. If you only need one car, you either fix it or replace it.

One of the advantages of the public enterprise form was that its terms and conditions of operation could be set directly by government. The evidence is growing that when these operations are privatised the state's role becomes more, rather than less, complex. This is because public utilities usually operate in markets which are characterised by natural monopoly. The fixed costs of laying an optical fibre cable, or a railway track, or a major water pipe are very high, so that once an investment is made, it is almost impossible for another firm to enter the market. Competition is possible only if the incumbent firm is forced to allow other firms to access the network. Establishing the terms on which this might be done requires the setting up of regulatory bodies which must exercise the wisdom of Solomon in creating the elusive level playing field.

Yet the skills needed to make the new kind of state work are being eroded. Cuts to departments and agencies are not getting rid of dead wood, but the best people: those who can see some hope of making a living elsewhere. Expertise is being leached away. How can the state be an effective regulator or even an intelligent customer when the specialists are all in the private sector? Those who remain grow tired and resentful. You can push dedicated people into running things on a shoestring because they are doing work they love and which they believe to be important. But eventually, frayed shoestrings break.

The independence and probity of public officials have been undermined by American-style purges as governments change and as public service boards have lost their central role in maintaining the structure of a career service. As a result, politicians in Australia enjoy more unfettered power than at any time in our history. Paranoia if not paralysis is rife within Senior Executive Services. Agencies caught up in power politics cannot do their jobs well. In this case, we have imported American practice, but not the offsetting checks and balances provided by a division of power between executive and legislature.

It used to be the case that many of the country's ablest people went into the public sector not because they wanted cushy jobs, but because they saw the opportunity to build worthwhile careers. Bright young graduates still apply to join Australian public services, but increasingly they spend no more than a few years working for government before leaving to join the private sector. The experience looks good on your CV but to stay too long would be fatal. When the axe falls, you've got nowhere to go.

Sooner or later, the lack of a viable public sector will start to have an impact on the public and on business. It will also affect the politicians now carrying out their work of destruction. Policy-making capacity deteriorates when there is no longer a core of able and experienced public servants to 'road-test' new ideas, and ministers rely instead on young and often inexperienced personal advisers, or consultants, for practical advice. Some time (one assumes before the next election) they will realise that if they are going to do something positive for this country, they will need experienced public servants to make it work.

One of the most intriguing questions is why all this happened. Economic rationalism established itself within the organs of the state and took over political parties not because it was rational, but because it was convenient. A minimalist state lets government off the hook. You don't have to worry about the public interest, because the market is supposedly taking care of it. If the industry is a regulated one, the public can take its complaints to the regulator. If not, there are always the courts. Supporters of deregulated economics tend to be those with the assets, information and know-how to take advantage of them – useful allies for any political party.

What of the opposition? If, as I have argued, economic rationalism represents a fundamental unravelling of key distributive arrangements in the Australian state, we would expect it to be vigorously opposed from many quarters, and from the political left in particular. There have been voices raised in protest, but they have come from small business people and manufacturers rather than unionists; from populists rather than radicals and from the Democrats and, increasingly the Greens, rather than the ALP.

The academic left largely ignored the industry policy issue throughout the 1970s. Academics were interested in feminism, environmentalism, gay rights, Aboriginal land rights – all important issues, but as the ALP found in 1996, not ones which cut much ice with ordinary Australians. Too many people were looking the other way as the core Australian idea – that the state supported you through your job, not with fancy sorts of retraining once you were out of work – was lost.

The role and attitudes of the union movement are more difficult to explain. The leadership of the union movement was persuaded to endorse economic rationalism through its accord with the ALP. Just what the leadership of the ACTU got for its forbearance is difficult to see. When the story of the 1980s is told from a vantage point further removed than our own, historians will find it difficult to understand why the unions at that time signed what proved to be their own death warrants.

Whatever benefits the various Accords generated flowed to non-unionists as well as to union members. Not only did the membership of unions contract; they failed to recruit in new areas of the workforce. The leaders of the labour movement agreed to a wholly inadequate industry policy because they bought Paul Keating's nonsense about exports saving the day and because they believed the Accord guaranteed equality of opportunity through health and education spending. They failed to understand that destroying the traditional industry policy was only part of a larger agenda. In this agenda, public investment is seen as always being less efficient than private. Forms of co-operation are always inferior to competition, and planning of any kind is an anathema. Government and its works are dead weight – the lead in the saddle-bags, as Canberra economist and academic Ross Garnaut is fond of saying.

This is a fundamentally unsound way of viewing any political economy. Whether as a regulator or as an owner, the state remains the most powerful means we have of articulating a collective interest in the economic life of the nation. If it fails to perform this function, or is even believed to be failing, it loses legitimacy. When sufficient citizens start to think that their society is no longer run fairly, even the best-entrenched regimes will not prevail. That should give even the most single-minded reformer pause.

THE MAN IN THE GREY CARDIGAN

My first boss in the public service taught me many things – where to find a policy; how to write a letter; how to manage a file. He arrived punctually in the office every morning, took off his coat, and put on a grey cardigan which he kept on a hanger behind the door. He was a man of the utmost regularity – he took his toilet breaks at exactly the same time each day.

It would be easy to make fun of him and others like him, yet the public really did have a servant in him. There was little he did not know, could not remember or was unsure of. He would not bend the rules for anyone.

He was not a man to head an organisation, and even in those distant times before public sector management was invented, this was well understood. But he was a loyal lieutenant to our ultimate boss, a genial man with a mind as sharp as a tack and a consummate skill at getting people to agree with each other, known to everyone as 'Jack'.

It was in watching Jack run meetings that I realised how much a good chairperson could accomplish. In the years since, as I have sat, frustrated, in countless meetings while poorly prepared or intransigent people wasted their own and everyone else's time, I have often wished he would reappear and sort things out.

Jack would talk to anyone in the organisation, which was usually held to be evidence of his democratic style. But I think now that he was picking up information, sizing people up, while appearing to be passing the time of day. On one of these occasions, I remember Jack told me he disliked travel because he never knew what he was going to have for his dinner, an attitude I found incomprehensible at the time, but am now beginning to understand. I hope he enjoyed his retirement.

As for my boss in the grey cardigan, I imagine he has been packaged out of the new public service long since. He and his type would be regarded as living fossils, relics of an earlier era.

The Commonwealth public service I remember from those days – stable, capacious, careful – has gone forever, but it is difficult to get a feel for what has taken its place. There are fewer public servants than before but, in many areas, the jobs have simply shifted into the private sector as functions have been outsourced.

As the ubiquitous Professor Fels (former head of the Australian Competition and Consumer Commission) continually reminded us, government in the age of deregulation is as busy as ever, and whichever party is in power, increasingly bossy and intrusive. There are more rules than ever, but somehow they don't make us feel safer, or happier. People are working harder, which is no bad thing, but they have a slightly desperate air, as if the constant managerial churning to which they are subject saps, rather than releases, energy.

Public servants are used to being compared, adversely, with their counterparts in the private sector. No one is supposed to let on that many government jobs, even those at relatively lowly levels, are actually quite interesting. Many involve a public policy or facilitation element which gives a degree of variety and intellectual challenge rare in private sector jobs. Public service is no longer a career in the way it was, but where departments are intelligently led, there are opportunities for training, experience and self-development. New graduate recruits, for example, are not, as my generation tended to be, regarded as slaves to the photocopier but as assets to be wooed and retained. Their continuing commitment can no longer be taken for granted, so the public service must work harder to keep them.

The new public service rarely writes down what it thinks it is doing. There just isn't the time. Messages are electronic and ephemeral. (When a computer virus called the 'love bug' did the rounds of the large bureaucracies, rumour has it that only the departments of Prime Minister and Cabinet and Finance were immune. They knew that a message headed 'I love you' could not be intended for them.)

While there are meetings galore, the minutes, if any, are a perfunctory affair. My old boss, who was meticulous about documenting every conceivably relevant occurrence, would have been horrified. Central registries, which opened and kept track of files in an orderly fashion, have long gone. Far from being an object of reverence, the files are a distraction from the ongoing business of being businesslike.

Now that the government has flogged off to the private sector most of the buildings it used to own, departments change premises a lot more than they used to, chasing cheaper rents. I believe this is called cost effectiveness. But at every move, a few more of the files disappear, never get unpacked or are 'accidentally' thrown out. Archivists must weep tears of blood. But public service departments see themselves as businesses, and businesses don't keep much in the way of records.

Rather than staying in the one job, public servants now move around a lot. This used to be frowned upon, a bit like being married too many times. Departmental structures were relatively rigid, as the principle that the person and the job were separate entities (a safeguard against nepotism) was still firmly established. Public servants held an 'office' (in practice a particular position, with a classification and salary attached to it) to which they were appointed, and if you wanted to move, you had to find an 'office' to move to. Now, with the concept of office abandoned, agency Heads can have as few (or as many) positions within their budgetary limits as they like, which makes for a much more flexible workforce.

Unfortunately all this flexibility creates problems when no one can remember how the job is supposed to be done. Noticing this, the consultants have dreamed up something called 'knowledge management'. Just as asset management has become necessary as departments have lost their assets, so knowledge management has become necessary now that many are not quite sure what they are doing.

The same thing seems to have happened with what are now called 'public service values'. These are principles of political neutrality, merit-based employment, the giving of frank advice to politicians and subscribing to the highest ethical standards. When the old Public Service Act, first legislated in 1922, was replaced in 1999, great importance was attached to the fact that the new Act listed the values explicitly, a sure sign that their survival was threatened. I never heard my old boss speak about ethics. I doubt that it would have occurred to him that acting properly was something that you needed to be reminded of.

Departments no longer feel much sense of pride in belonging to government. Indeed, many public servants talk of 'government' as though they had nothing to do with it. One agency I know has even got rid of the kangaroo and emu from its letterhead. They have been replaced by a logo. You know the sort of thing—a stylised picture with arrows going around it, or through it, so as to indicate purposeful activity. The public sector differs irrevocably from the private in one respect: people in the private sector do not have professional politicians for bosses. The political bosses purport to run the entire show, but in practice remain in total ignorance of almost everything that goes on within departments. This ignorance has many advantages, not the least of which is that ministers always have someone else to blame when things go wrong.

Public servants, on the other hand, pretend that 'the minister' decides almost everything. This is a most convenient fiction, because it means that when things go wrong, they too have someone else to blame. In practice, neither the minister nor the public servants have as much power as they think they do, because the communication between them is controlled by the minister's advisers. These 'meretricious players' as then Secretary to the Treasury John Stone once famously referred to them, are chosen because they share the same political prejudices as the minister. But they are usually inexperienced, and have very little understanding of the complexities of planning and implementation.

Politics, of course, is as powerful a force as ever. Politicians still want to be re-elected, and they usually spend money to do it, or at least they promise to do so. The irony is that the years of fiscal stringency have probably made them even more irresponsible – a bit like a dieter who, having reached the target, binges on Big Macs and chocolate.

When I studied public administration in the early 1980s, we used to worry a lot about politicisation. The public service was meant to be apolitical. It wasn't, of course, but neutrality was believed to be at least a plausible idea, a concept to which subscription was possible without hypocrisy on the one hand, or naivete on the other. There was also acknowledgment that, in the business of appearing to decide what to do about problems, there is a lot of hard yakka involved, researching causes, costs and implications. That is the work of experienced people. I have noticed that in universities, particularly the smaller ones, how management often flounders because there are too few people to make sense of what is going on, to work out the key issues that need attention and to help devise plans for addressing them.

If governments, anywhere, were serious about policy, they would hoard people with this kind of skill as if they were the rarest of treasures. The previous Labor government, to give it credit, was reasonably skilled at creating environments in which people could bring these skills to bear. The current Coalition government seems much more uncomfortable about using what is on offer. This probably reflects its perception of the effects of Labor's moulding of the public service. Once begun, politicisation is irreversible, as each new government throws out the appointees of its predecessor.

Like most of the really interesting developments in our society, politicisation attracts little serious discussion. It was discussed far more when there was less of it around. Top public servants know they will last only so long as they retain the minister's confidence. This means they will keep their jobs until even the journalists notice that something is wrong.

Senior public servants must learn to read and interpret political windshifts as never before. But it is as managers, we are told, that they must now be judged. The new framework of public management pretends that public servants have clearly defined goals, and sufficient flexibility to determine the way they are achieved. Yet in any real sense, they probably manage less than was the case a decade ago. It is not uncommon, in the Canberra bureaucracy, for middle managers to have no subordinates at all. This is not because everything has been outsourced, but because the shape of the average department is no longer pyramidal, but diamond-shaped. There are fewer jobs at the bottom, and about the same number at the top, while those in the middle have expanded significantly in number.

Technology has made jobs more alike – documents are generated by two-finger typists rather than by professional word processor operators. But there has clearly been a far harsher pruning of the more menial positions than those higher up the hierarchy. The result is that the level of pay, per unit of responsibility, has greatly increased.

One of the biggest misconceptions is that managers are managing for observable outputs and outcomes. On the face of it, doing things which produce worthwhile results is what public sector management should be all about. It is just that no one, least of all the politicians, is fair dinkum about finding ways of doing it. The language of reporting has changed, not that of organisational life. The public sector continues to be driven by the imperatives of the moment. As one senior British civil servant said, 'We don't produce an output, we get the job done.'

It would be wrong to romanticise the old public services. They were often over-manned, overly bureaucratic and insufficiently attuned to the needs of their clients. The point is that no change is made without costs, and no one, it seems, is inclined to acknowledge the fact.

The financially trained persons who have constructed most of the edifice of new public management assume that public servants are, or should be, motivated by money. Performance pay and bonuses of various kinds are paid to those who have achieved agreed targets. But what makes any organisation tick is not money – it is challenge, fulfilment. The best managers in the private sector understand this. It is the public sector's misfortune to have been enveloped not by a private sector ethos, but by politicians' impressions of what the private sector is like.

The effects on morale, motivation and commitment have

been considerable. Public service cannot be reduced to management, because there will always be constraints on what public servants can actually do. The best departments will encourage an entrepreneurship of information and ideas, which in turn requires daring, not conformity, and a cool-eyed rather than a timorous attitude to risk.

Much that should not have changed, or should have been changed in different ways, has been torn down. Edmund Burke's advice is surely apposite here: 'it is with infinite caution that any man ought to venture upon pulling down an edifice which answered in any tolerable degree the common purposes of society.'

It is interesting that State governments, which led the way with hard-edged financial management and novel outsourcings, are slowly reconsidering. Splitting organisations is fine in theory. Making some purchasers and others providers promises greater accountability. In practice, the loss of communication far outweighs any efficiencies. The key problem is not how many public servants there are, but what happens to those who cannot or will not do their jobs properly. It is still far too easy for those who wish to, to evade responsibility simply by not doing anything. A principal of a government school said to me that his job was hard, but what made it hard was not a lack of resources, but the fact that he could not get rid of sub-standard teachers. Everyone knew who they were, but there was no money for semi-forced redundancies. The education department spread the pain by shifting the dud teachers from one school to the next.

But you don't know what you've got til it's gone. 'We never knew how important Grandpa was,' said a friend, 'until he died and Grandma went off and joined the scientologists.' So it was with the Australian state. It was a patchwork of almost impenetrable cross subsidies, a sort of socialism without state ownership. It made possible, even encouraged, enormous inefficiencies. But at least it had a clear foundation in popular values, an understanding of political economy which saw equity as being secured through production, rather than handouts. What, in terms of those fundamental ideals, are we doing now?

The public sector is out of fashion, and at least at the national level likely to remain so, not because there is a compelling case against doing things through government, but because we no longer have a clear idea about what government is for. Every time a function that used to be performed by public servants is outsourced to the private sector, private jobs substitute for public ones. They are much the same jobs, but because public servants are invisible employees, it feels like we are ahead.

Let's face it, the bottom line looks so much more impressive when the private sector is involved. Every time a government business is sold (and it is only the profitable ones that are put on the block), there is a small fortune to be made by private financial consultants, underwriters and tax specialists. The mums and dads of Australia – beguiled by the rentier's vision of painless profits, or perhaps just looking for a safe place for their precious savings – acquire their parcel of shares. Now they are interested in Telstra in a way that was scarcely imaginable when they owned it as citizens, rather than investors. When the dividends went to government, they were invisible. Now they are the common gossip of the business pages.

'Making visible' the public's stake in public hospitals, schools and community services is not so easy to do. It is possible to value the physical and financial assets and publish the dollar figure in a balance sheet and in fact this is now routinely done, for hospitals at least. But the true stake the public has in these institutions is in the service they provide, and the expertise and traditions they have built up over the years, rather than their financial performance. By applying accounting methods devised for the private sector to the public sector, governments are encouraged to forget all but the financial side of stewardship.

The provision of education, telecommunications, transport, hospitals, community services – the 'infrastructure' of the economy – requires some kind of collective effort. The argument is not so much whether, but how, and when, government should be involved. Private companies look to governments to take a lead, because even the biggest of them cannot afford to take the risk of going it alone without public coordination and planning. When governments refuse to act as well, the result is that good projects go unfunded. The fact that, a century after federation, there is still no direct rail link between Sydney, Canberra and Melbourne is nothing short of scandalous.

At the heart of all this confusion is a deep-seated ambivalence about government which runs deep in the Australian psyche. There is a distaste for politics which makes all Australians natural public choice theorists. We expect failure in public life, and are perversely gratified when, unfailingly, it occurs.

We have never, by international standards, had a particularly 'big' government. Nor have we had government which has, by international standards, been inept. Yet we are not very proud of what government has achieved, even though government is just another name for our political selves.

We have grown used to the idea that government is there as a safety net, to catch those who are unable to gouge out a place for themselves in the globalising economy. This creates a situation which is quite unhealthy for any polity – government as the agent of redistribution, and not much else. Neither political party offers much that is different here, but the Liberals cater more completely to the growing tide of unreconstructed mean-ness which characterises those who believe they've 'made it' and those who wish they had.

Public schools and public health are for the poor. The unemployed, the indigent and the sick are policed by a large centralised bureaucracy which monitors their every move, a sort of electronic workhouse which speaks the language of customer service while 'breaching' (removing from benefits) those who fail to conform.

If you happen to be middle class and employed, government does not want to know about you, except to clobber you with income and consumption taxes which it will use to police the underclass, finance its vast regulatory apparatus and distribute largesse at election time. You must finance your own health, your kids' schooling and your retirement. You may as well not vote, because government has metaphorically kissed you goodbye. Yet government used to be for us, too.

As an average middle-class Australian, my life would have been immeasurably the poorer without government. I went to a government school which I hated at the time, and which contained several teachers who would have been better suited to employment as concentration camp attendants. But I learned how to parse a sentence, what the base pairs of DNA were, and I can still remember most of my French irregular verbs.

I went to school on a government-owned train, banked with a government-owned bank (the Commonwealth – remember the tin money box in the shape of the Martin Place head office?), and listened regularly to government-owned TV and radio. I don't think it occurred to anyone that these were not legitimate activities for governments to undertake, and as far as I know, while politics was never far away, governments did not despise the institutions which they owned and operated on behalf of the public.

I felt, and still feel, a genuine affection for the ABC, even though much of its relevance and bite has been worn away by incompetent and foolish management and stifled by political correctness. If it were shut down, or died of neglect, I would miss it.

I got an inkling of what life without the ABC might be like when, travelling in the United States for the first time, I was astounded to find that there was no state-owned broadcasting and that public television was funded by sponsors and by subscriptions. I will never forget my amazement when, half-way through a telecast of a very good production of *Romeo and Juliet*, the two lead actors appeared, still in their stage clothes, in a special segment in which they solicited donations to keep the station going.

Of course, Americans are mystified by Australian attitudes, too. They like the fact that we are not an armed camp, but find themselves nonplussed by middle-class Australians' timidity, conservatism and passivity. 'A colonial socialist dump' one acquaintance termed it, before reluctantly heading back home again. 'No one would do anything without asking permission first.' Those Americans who stay do very well here, because they have far more chutzpah (especially the women) than is considered seemly in the native-born.

The propensity to regard government as 'them', with a resigned sort of indifference, probably dates back to the convict era. In my childhood, we used to think that 'they' would fix up our problems for us; now we think 'they' are probably not much good for anything. Despite all the downsizings, a good proportion of the population is still employed by government but its actual operations remain as distant and mysterious as ever. This was brought home to me when as an academic in Canberra, I attempted to teach adolescents, many of them the sons and daughters of Commonwealth public servants, about the state. I asked them what their parents did. No one had a clue. Their mums and dads may as well have inhabited the planet Mars.

The Achilles heel of Australian government has always been the relationship between local, state and federal levels. For much of the post-war era, and in particular since the 1970s, the political class has not taken much interest in the states, still less in local government. While the states stagnated, Canberra flourished. Throughout that time, there was really only one political idea – whatever it was, Canberra should do it.

When change came, as it usually does, it affected the poorest and weakest first. Once the largesse of the Whitlam years had gone, the states were cut and cut again by the national government. They, in turn, cut everything they thought they could get away with. Now, like an auto-immune disease, the national government is attacking itself.

As far as I know, no one has ever asked the citizens what they want from their public service. Speaking personally, I would look for honesty, efficiency and competence. I do not think there are many Australians who believe that whatever the task, the private sector will perform it more efficiently, effectively and responsively than the public sector.

The problem is how to modernise public sector organisations so that they are more responsive to the needs of the communities they serve. In the days of the Coombs Commission, before economic thinking dominated everything, this was a problem believed to be solvable within the existing ethos of the public service, rather than one which required an elaborate machinery of quasi-market incentives and penalties to bring it about.

There will always be a need for organisations which do not have to serve the interests of their shareholders. Mutual organisations were created to serve the interests of members, that is people who both 'owned' the organisation, and were its customers. Co-operatives have the same idea, although in their case, it is the suppliers who are also the owners.

We should encourage not just varieties of activity, but

varieties of organisation. At the moment, we are restricting the capacity of many of our organisations by forcing them to converge – the public sector must become more business-like, while the private sector finds that it is required to act in more bureaucratic ways to conform to societal expectations. Not-for-profit organisations, recently – God help them – discovered by governments as all-purpose service deliverers, are becoming more like government. The impulse which turned Australia Post outlets into not very good newsagents and the Salvos into a large employment agency is surely to be deplored.

In parts of the world where almost everything is hopelessly corrupt, non-governmental, humanitarian organisations offer the only reliable means of getting help to where it is needed. But for many centuries in the west, religious and benevolent organisations operated hospitals, hostels and schools, and in general, they didn't do a very good job of it. As the state gradually took over, matters began to improve. To cause public money to flow through not-for-profit agencies, which are often far less skilled and accountable than the public sector they displaced, is surely a retrograde step, and one which will undermine the distinctive ethos of these organisations.

Similarly, the ethos of the public sector is compromised when it tries to imitate the private sector. Top public servants have many skills, but they are not businesspeople. Top public servants are networkers, diplomats and analysts. An acquaintance of mine, a consultant who makes a living teaching business executives how to 'work a room' and hold their knives properly, once told me that departmental secretaries needed no instruction in these arts. But, he added, they are not necessarily expert in the business of running things.

We know that the marketplace is very far from being self-regulating or even self-energising. Yet we seem helpless before the relentless forces of international business – the scale economies, market power and technology which engulf local initiative and drive large organisations to become ever larger. In this environment, which threatens to become an organisational monoculture, we need the equilibrating role and diverse values of the public sector as never before. Perhaps, for the same reasons, we need the man in the grey cardigan, not because we can turn him into something he is not, but because he represents a part of our organisational selves we cannot afford to lose.

THE POLITICS OF PLACE

My sister wrote recently from England, where she has lived for many years. When, she asked, rather plaintively, did I think global warming would start to take effect, because she didn't think she could stand another English summer.

I must say I feel a bit the same about globalisation. Ever since I first heard the word I have been waiting for globalisation to change my life in new and interesting ways, but the signs so far are not encouraging. Everywhere you look, the world seems to be in much the same mess as it always was. The only thing that changes is the location of the latest disaster. Still, something important seems to be going on, if only we could work out what it is.

'It's that weather program on CNN,' said someone. 'You know – the one where they give the forecast for everywhere all at once.' As I refuse on principle to pay to watch television, I had to wait until I was staying in a motel to find this program. But when I did, I was immediately hooked. Here was weather on a truly global scale.

It appears that the weather starts from somewhere near Mongolia and keeps on going from there. The presenters really get into the motions of all this weather, flinging their arms about and getting quite excited. But the forecasts are inclined to be broad-brush. From the satellite it may appear as if whole continents are in for a fine day. It makes it a bit difficult to figure out whether or not to take your brolly if you're walking down to the shops.

It is said that McDonald's is an indicator of globalisation. Indeed this hapless operation, whose only crime seems to have been to sell hamburgers without beetroot (and even that has recently been rectified) seems to come in for an inordinate amount of attention from the people who protest about things. There was even a French farmer, some sort of champion of the French way of eating, who tried to burn down his local McDonald's.

I have some trouble believing this man to be a hero. Traditional French cuisine was no doubt fabulous, but it enslaved generations of women to the tedium of daily shopping at street markets, and hours spent getting the roux just right. French eating habits are just not family-friendly. Kids don't like spending a couple of hours over lunch, and if you're travelling, most want to eat well before 8 pm. But no French chef can be persuaded to put on his apron, let alone cook you a meal, before that hour.

In these circumstances, it is hardly surprising that French families seem to find McDonald's just as useful a place to take the kids as Australian families do. Nor is it true that McDonald's offerings are the same everywhere. In Paris the McDonald's breakfast comes with a quite respectable crepe with maple syrup. And the coffee isn't bad either.

McDonald's are supposed to look the same everywhere. But that is not true, either. In the sixth arrondissement, McDonald's is housed in a very suave late nineteenth-century building, its golden arches reduced to two pairs of modest yellow parentheses attached to the first floor balcony.

Perhaps being big is bad in itself? I cannot see there is any moral difference between Smith Kline Beecham and somebody knocking up herbal cures in their garage. Presumably

both are trying to make a bob or two. Indeed, the drugs produced by the major pharmaceutical companies are far more
regulated than so-called natural products, many of which
contain quite alarming substances. If you are prescribed a pill
made by a drug company, you can be sure that it is better
than a placebo by a statistically significant margin. You might,
as I do, secretly hanker after the placebo, but then if you
knew it was a placebo it would presumably no longer work.

With large companies, too, you have the added reassur-
ance of knowing that any exploitation of the consumer has
been done well in advance of the point of sale. Small business, on the other hand, is inclined to make it up as it goes
along. In many countries, mysterious charges can be almost
guaranteed to proliferate on the bill at the corner restaurant,
whereas the employees at the local transnational corporation
know they must charge you what's on the menu.

Some successful companies are now starting to pride themselves on how ethical they are. I have no idea what all those
jars in the Body Shop are actually for, but at least I know their
contents have not been tested on animals. Dick Smith has been
criticised for using Aussie ownership as a marketing device,
but at least he gives some of his profits to charity. Where will
it all end? Will big business be shamed into helping out in
developing countries, even as the governments of developed
countries get meaner and meaner? One of the many ironies of
globalisation is that nations think of themselves as businesses,
while corporations become more and more like governments.

Pressing though these problems are, many of them have a
familiar ring. I seem to recall, in my youth, protesting against
transnational companies which behaved badly in Latin
America. On balance, I would have said the firms have
cleaned up their acts a bit in the years since, or have simply
exited countries which cause them trouble. It is governments which have become worse.

No, if globalisation has any meaning at all, it must be a result of technological change. Forget the thousands of people sitting at their home computers hoping that they will find the meaning of life on the internet, if only it would work a bit faster. Technology makes it possible, if you are employed by a large bank or hedge fund, to trade, day and night, in a bewildering array of financial assets.

These great tides of money, washing in and out of exchanges and trading places around the world, either inundate governments or leave them high and dry. Transactions, many of them undertaken automatically by computer, take place in markets which know neither national nor geographical boundaries, and determine, at least in the short term, the price of currencies, the value of shares and bonds, and much else besides.

I am told that these markets are operated by members of transnational elites, people who have no allegiance to any one place or country, but are citizens of Ernst and Young, or IBM. Recruited young (and the competition is keen), they remain honoured citizens of these 'countries' until there is a downturn, or they are no longer useful. There is little room for sentiment, and less for loyalty, in the global marketplace.

But the national marketplace is much the same. Global trade reproduces between nations what already happens within them. It is the force which, relentlessly, pitches those without market power against those with it. Countries can be without market power, and so can people. If you are a factory worker, a local manager, a lower level bureaucrat, you are a loser from globalisation.

Knowledge workers imagine that they are immune, but in fact many of them could be next in line: whatever can be centralised can be globalised. It would be a simple matter, for example, to put me, a teacher, out of a job. By enrolling in a virtual university, Australian students could sign on to the lectures of someone who was internationally famous. The only thing hampering such a development is assessment: it would be almost impossible to say whether the person answering the questions online is actually the person who is enrolled in the degree. But perhaps, as long as someone pays, no one really cares about that any more.

Capitalism, as Marx foretold, destroys all local allegiances and attachments. Football teams used to come from particular parts of a country, or a city. Blokes you knew were out on the field, and you supported your team whether it won or lost. Indeed there was a sort of resigned pride in turning out, year after year, for a side which seemed always to be up against players who were bigger, stronger and faster than your own. (Parents of junior footballers may still be experiencing this phenomenon.)

Now football teams are business enterprises, and profitable only if they win most of the time, or have access to rivers of poker machine money. To ensure that they win, club managements buy and sell players from all over the world. With millions of fans worldwide, Manchester United has become the world's first global football team. In playing this colossus on their home ground, the Singapore national team found that it had fewer supporters than the opposition.

Of course, eventually, the most successful clubs become too successful, and the clubs which do not win start to wither and die. Someone has to start evening things out again, or the competition on which all depends is itself destroyed. As with football clubs, so with citizens, regions and countries.

Without political development, market economies cannot flourish. The people of poor countries are poor not because they cannot export bananas to Europe (although no doubt that would help), but because they are not fully functional political communities. That was the real achievement of nations and nation-building – an intricate interweaving of the economic and the political, which determined the basis for generating and sharing national wealth.

Nation states are said to be no match for the power of global capital, and their demise as active players on the world stage is widely prophesied. This may be true, but in the case of developed countries at least, there is a long way to go. Nobody seems to have told the Americans that their government is headed for irrelevance.

Even developing countries are far from helpless. The rainforests of the Solomon Islands are being devastated by Malaysian logging companies not because the government of the Solomons is powerless, but because it is corrupt, incompetent and, of course, broke.

Most investment by global firms is not in the developing, but the developed, world. It is not easy to do business in places where the local elites are on the take, there is no independent judiciary to settle disputes, and where it is difficult to find trained people. BHP came unstuck over Ok Tedi not because it was an evil company, but because the PNG government did a deal it was not entitled to transact. When you sell someone another person's livelihood, you are asking for trouble.

The nation state, so often portrayed as superfluous, is in fact necessary for trade. This is for two reasons. Firstly, nation states compensate the losers among their own citizens, after a fashion. Unalloyed free trade invariably destroys the political system on which it is based, because even if the winners win more than the losers lose, the losers will not, in the long run, accept the situation. Why should they? If equity is neglected, the dispossessed will use the political system to redress the situation – where they can.

Secondly, and more controversially, nation states segregate citizens of low wage and high wage countries. Without this segregation, there would be much less world trade, because citizens of low wage countries would simply move to the richer countries, up until the point where the differences between them were evened out. As the world contains some very poor countries, the living standards faced by new arrivals in wealthy countries would have to be very low indeed before migration became uneconomic.

Wealthy communities have always been a target for those 'on the outside' and, historically, have invariably been overwhelmed sooner or later, which is why residents of developed nations feel threatened by new, unwanted arrivals, whether they admit to it or not. Wealthy countries want to play both ends against the middle – accept sufficient people to keep their labour markets healthy, but continue to buy the cheap goods that low wages elsewhere make possible.

It is the poor, the dispossessed and the ambitious who move. Unless they have good reasons to leave, most people stay in the same country, many in the same city or even the same town, in which they were born. Australians are no exception. We move house a lot (trading up to real estate heaven), but we tend not to go very far. Two of my neighbours grew up less than 500 metres from where they now live (closer to Mum, I think, for babysitting purposes). When attending a recent school reunion, I was surprised how many of my contemporaries were living close to where we had all gone to school, perhaps because they had inherited their parents' houses, perhaps because there seemed no real reason to move.

Of those who leave their birthplace, some never come back. In the case of expatriates such as Germaine Greer this is probably just as well – she can annoy us just as effectively from 10,000 miles away, anyway. But many do come back, concerned that their children will miss out on something important if they do not grow up in Australia, or having reached a point of eminence from which they can practise their profession anywhere.

Others ostensibly migrate, but find it difficult to live in Australia and make money at the same time. We see evidence of flags of convenience everywhere. In parts of Sydney there is a fashion for building enormous homes right to the boundary line of the property. Many of these edifices are owned by Chinese businesspeople who live in them only occasionally, while they pursue business opportunities in Hong Kong and Taiwan. Locals call their residences 'dark houses'. There is no one there, except for the occasional visits of the housekeeper.

Firms can move now, too, although in Australia's case, it is always in one direction – off shore. To be transnational is no longer enough. Global reach demands that even a company as large and diverse as BHP must cede control to a relative parvenu like Billiton. But we have learned to be philosophical about these things. Power and control move inexorably to the more populous and capital-rich parts of the world, but while we in Australia have the resources the rest of the world needs, who cares? No one can take them from us, or so we like to think.

As Australians, our wealth relates to the land we live on in a very direct way. We will never be a knowledge nation or even a clever country, but if we have sufficient will and imagination, we may be one of the first developed countries to rebuild the idea of the nation state from the bottom up, from the point of view of the land itself.

What is our country? The environmentalists' slogan 'think globally, act locally' seems to overlook the need to think locally, as well. Political boundaries are not much help here. It is difficult to identify with a Local Government Area. A river catchment or geographic region makes more sense, except that regionalism has never been very strong in Australia. Do people identify with the 'Sunshine Coast', or the other creations of regional marketing? Somehow I doubt it. If we try hard enough, we may come to understand more about 'country' in the Aboriginal sense. But as the sports commentators say, it is a big ask.

One of the displays at the National Museum of Australia (which is a fine place to visit, as long as it stays free), features the Anbarra people. The Anbarra live in the north of Australia, on an estuary on the northern coast of Arnhem Land. This is an intricate coastline, virtually unknown to most Australians. There is a map within the display showing the sacred sites, each of which has an association with a particular wangarr, or creation spirit. The creation spirits included the kingfisher, water goanna and flounder. I do not pretend to understand much about the relationship between the Anbarra and their land, but I imagine that the animals which live in it, and the places which bear their names, constitute a way of 'seeing' landscape.

After spending many hours in front of traditional Aboriginal paintings wondering what on earth they were about, I liked this display because it seemed to explain traditional Aboriginal ways of seeing the world in a way that made some sort of sense to me. By understanding the relationship between the flat land along the coast, the great tidal river and its tributaries cutting into it, and the location of the sacred sites, it was possible to begin to make a translation from a western depiction of the world to one that is based on a more immediate horizon and a quite different sense of what is important. For the Anbarra people the land was about food, as it must have been to all our ancestors.

Settling in one place does not really change the equation – it simply fixes the frame more precisely. Even when Europeans began to turn themselves into farmers, and invented various forms of personal gods whose sacred sites could be constructed where humans encountered the deity, rather than where the deity was presumed to live, they must have been alive to the rhythms of the land – their lives depended on it.

I imagine that farmers and graziers, at least those still living on the land, must feel a strong attachment to it. But those of us living in cities and suburbs see place quite differently. We buy houses, or at least most people do, because of their location: close to shops and schools. Quiet street. But the main criterion is that the other houses in the street must be of sufficient grandeur to enhance our own.

The land has disappeared under rose bushes, roads and car parks. We see it in the distance – it is what we call a view. The early explorers traversed and named the country – we transform it with our pace of travel. Before the double highway between Canberra and Sydney was built, there were large sections of the road which were single lane each way. The road followed the contours of the landscape. Climbing the Razorback and descending the other side, mounting the gap between Lake George and the hills leading to Canberra. Eucalypts on either side caught and held the sun.

Now the freeway claims the landscape. There are parts of it which are intensely beautiful, like the enormous viaducts to the east of Mittagong. Passing Goulburn, you can see over to the old brewery and, beside it, the chain of ponds which led the early settlers to choose this site for a town. But we do not stop for a cup of tea, as we might once have done when the road took us down the main street.

Where is our country? Many of us live in houses with gardens which reflect the seasons and climate. But these patches of land are not 'country'. When I see the sun set behind the Brindabellas, I think of that curious pattern of silhouette and blue shadow as mine in some way, and I would hate to see its beauty marred. Perhaps that feeling is the beginnings of country.

We pay a price for everything. What we have lost (and in the case of white Australians never had) is the ability to see a landscape as the sole source of our being. Everything we

consume comes, of course, from the soil, but modern production techniques have obscured the relationship totally.
Just about everything we consume, unless we are Italian and
have a vegie patch, comes from somewhere else.

When large areas of rural Australia are succumbing to
dryland salt, just as the irrigated areas of Victoria are beginning to drown in a rising, saline water table, it is difficult to
see the effects of our pattern of production, because most of
us live in cities. For white Australians, the dangers are particularly great because we alienate prime agricultural land in
the interests of home building – the one industry which all
Australian governments support.

A sense of economic place is also important. I always like
to know where the things I use come from. This can be a
chastening exercise for Australians when our shirts come
from China, our hedge clippers from Taiwan and our tinned
asparagus from Peru. But many people do not bother to
find out.

I have friends, both scientists, who live in Dallas, Texas.
They never, they told me, visit anywhere which does not
have a proper water supply and civilised hotels (I was not
game enough to tell them that, in my experience, this ruled
out large parts of America). They do not read the labels on
jars of fruit conserves or packets of cheese. They are not
much interested in where anything comes from, provided it
serves the purpose for which it was bought.

When I arrived to visit them for the first time, I was naturally interested in where they live. Dallas is a big, sprawling
city with a commercial centre homogenised by the relentless
forces of millennial capitalism. Yet surely it must have come
from somewhere. What was the history of Dallas? How did it
get there? My host did not know, did not care, even though
he had grown up in the place. It was a place that housed his
institution, his laboratory, his students. And that was that.

But Dallas cannot escape from its past. It will always bear the stigma of being the place where President Kennedy was assassinated. The city clearly does not know what to make of this embarrassing distinction. The event cannot easily be commemorated, yet how can it be left unacknowledged? For want of a better idea, the city has wisely left the curve of road taken by the motorcade, the grassy knoll and the Texas Book Depository much as they were.

It's a surprisingly intimate scene, the distances much smaller than I had imagined. Some local entrepreneurs had put up a sort of kiosk housing various kinds of ghoulish memorabilia, including graphic eyewitness descriptions. I realised, with a shock, how horrific the injuries that led to Kennedy's death must have been.

There is something very important about seeing a place 'in the flesh'. This is because the flesh that we see it with is our own. And because no photograph, no film, no virtual reality can give us the proportions, the feel, the smell of the original. An acquaintance who had grown up in Western Australia, which seems to sit entirely on sand, said that the first thing he noticed when he went to Tasmania was the smell of earth everywhere.

Globalisation clearly has something to do with the Americans discovering the rest of the world. While we Australians have known about foreigners for a very long time, until fairly recently, most Americans, except the small minority who invested in other countries, did not have much occasion to concern themselves with them. What other country calls the agency that is supposed to deal with people outside the United States, the State Department? Even the Brits have the decency to call their equivalent the Foreign Office.

Americans, at least the wealthier ones, travel in a way that is truly unique. I recall meeting a charming group in

Istanbul, all of whom had apparently been to Australia. Oh, we inquired, which bits of Australia? There was some discussion. They had certainly been to the Barrier Reef, but beyond that, it all got a bit vague. What were they planning to see in Istanbul? Again, no one was quite sure. Trying to be helpful, we suggested they take a tram ride to a famous shop, not far away, which had invented Turkish Delight. But where would they find a tram? We gave them a copy of our map, but it was clear they had no real use for it. They would find someone who would take them to the shop. And, of course, they did.

The Japanese do not travel so much as search for familiar things in unexpected situations. I will never forget, when visiting Young one hot recent summer, encountering several busloads of Japanese tourists visiting the local jam factory. The tour guide explained that they had come to see the cherry blossom or, failing that, the cherry trees. Why, I wondered, would Japanese people visit Young to see the cherry blossom when they had so much of it at home? Global travel has many mysteries.

In the battle between choice and standardisation, scale economies pull one way, and the human desire for variety pulls the other. Cars have different names, the result of some dictionary trawl by an Asian marketer (what on earth does 'Lantra' mean?) but they are basically much the same in appearance and performance. The cars of thirty years ago were much more idiosyncratic, in both good and bad ways. They certainly looked different – a Mini Minor and a Volkswagen were both small cars, but one could never be mistaken for the other. Now cars of the same size are much of a muchness.

But quality, or at least reliability, is much more apparent. That much, at least, the Japanese taught us before they began to disappear beneath the weight of the corporate state which brought them riches, but infantilised their culture and ultimately betrayed them.

As the Europeans have discovered, promoting trade in services requires much social engineering. Almost everything can be a barrier to trade – national legal systems, customs, culture, even language itself. After all, if the Japanese spoke English better than they do, it would make it easier for American companies to penetrate their markets without having to get the instruction manuals translated.

Language is one of the last repositories of difference. Because we speak the same language, more or less, as the British and the Americans, we Australians know what it is to grow up with other people's cultures in our head. We do not have the protection of language, a place to go that is truly our own, as Scandinavians or the French do.

As native speakers of the lingua franca, we run the risk of believing that those who use our language to communicate with us, use it in the same way as we do. Speaking English is a bit like learning to play the violin. Almost anyone can get a sound out of it, but to play it well takes a good ear and years of practice. Similarly, just about any non-English speaker can produce a few words. But it takes real commitment to use the language properly.

Am I for or against globalisation? It depends what you are globalising. Global developed-country living standards would be a good thing. So, probably, would global democracy, religious tolerance and fair treatment for minority groups. However global crime, global tourism and global movies do not appeal.

It may be that some of the good things are happening. But for the moment, we live in a world in which the level of dischrony – the huge differences in outlook and behaviour evident at the same time on the same planet – are becoming ever more marked.

To take an example from the recent past: in Afghanistan, the Taliban – the Daleks of the modern era – banned the importation of products with images on them, because images are anathema in the Koran. At the same time, a woman in France gave birth, at the age of nearly 60, to a child of which she was not the biological mother, but the biological father was her own brother. Take your pick.

But then, a homogeneous world is not all together attractive, either. The fact that somebody in Bombay might be ringing me up trying to sell me something, possibly even my own house, does not thrill me. The fact that the central business districts of cities everywhere look increasingly alike does not excite me. In a truly global world, just as the immortal (and eternally young) inhabitants of the science fiction film *Zardoz* begged for death, so would the inhabitants of earth do anything to be different. Tourists do not, in general, want to spend money visiting places which look just like home (although it can always be diverting to find, in some out of the way place, the proverbial person from Wollongong). Indeed, the concern for heritage is less about keeping the past than it is about retaining sufficient differentness to interest the tourists.

When E.F. Schumacher published *Small is Beautiful* in 1973, it seemed to make a lot of sense. But global capitalism seems to have put paid to sustainable smallness, or even medium-size. We live in an age of extremes. The big firms keep on getting bigger and there are always plenty of small ones, although few small businesses last for very long. But there are few firms in the middle. They get taken over by the giants, or they disappear.

I would suggest, though, that sooner or later, bigness and distance start to become wearisome. Big-scale farming in Europe has proved to be an ecological and health disaster. When, because of the BSE scare, it became important to know where your meat came from, no one knew any more. What to do about it? It is all very well asking consumers to make a choice, to force producers to take heed. But business has become so complex, even the simplest products have components from somewhere else. It is hard to say whether an Australian-made shirt was produced in a factory where the workers are paid a decent wage, or not. Of two locally made versions of paracetamol, should we prefer the one made by an Australian-owned company? True, dividends are distributed here, but there is nothing to stop them going offshore again, if the recipients so choose.

Buying fresh does not really make the choices easier. I can have a factory chook produced in the ACT, but if I want a free-range one, it has to come from Queensland. My tomatoes come from the Darling Downs, and my milk from somewhere south of the Victorian border. The fish I buy at the fishmongers, even if it was caught off the South Coast, is first sucked up into the giant maw of Sydney before it is allowed to be sold in Canberra. Most of the enormous trucks that pound the highways of the nations night and day are probably carrying food.

I would prefer it if more of the food I eat were grown closer to home, but because a nation is by definition a customs union, and the internal movement of goods may not be impeded, there is not much that can be done politically to secure that result. Nor can my puny purchasing power do much to bring about change. In the game of market forces, as with politics, it is the numbers which count.

There are a few environmental heroes up in the hills, resolute in their homespun jumpers and grimly proud of their composting toilets. But most people will continue to do what is convenient, and buy what is cheapest. Whether a democratic society can, or even should, change any of that, is an open question.

VOLUNTEERING

It was the time of the last school fete. I had volunteered to run the bookstall, and it had just started to rain. As I struggled to cover the sprawling collection of ancient street directories, battered textbooks and assorted pamphlets that constituted our stock (the dealers had cleaned out the decent stuff at first light), I found my thoughts turning, somewhat unexpectedly, to the subject of social capital.

Social capital is the currently fashionable term for the goodwill and trust that people display towards each other in community life and which underpins their ability to cooperate with each other. As I heaved boxes of books around the now rain-spattered stall, I reflected that if all the people currently extolling the virtues of social capital actually contributed to its formation, we would have far less of a problem finding people to run the fete.

There just don't seem to be the numbers of volunteers that there used to be. While the actual number of community organisations remain as high as ever, the sports clubs, scout groups, even professional associations, are finding it harder and harder to find the public-spirited people who will keep them running. Everyone has a theory as to the reason, mostly of the 'world is going to pot' variety. 'People are more materialistic than they used to be,' said a friend in his sixties. Normally,

I would discount this kind of explanation, but in a society in which the major form of recreation (apart from watching sport) is shopping, he might have a point.

Academic research in the United States suggests that club membership is indeed on the decline across all socio-economic groups. The American academic David Putnam, after considering a number of possible explanations, blames the advent of television. He reaches this conclusion because the US data indicate that declining membership is generational, and first became manifest not in the 1990s, but in the 1970s. The generation born in the 1950s, the first to grow up with television, has proved significantly less civic-minded than the preceding generation. Television not only takes up time, but seems to privatise leisure.

Funnily enough, no one that I have approached on this matter says that they are too busy watching television to get involved in voluntary work. Everyone professes to be too busy doing other things, and indeed many are. These days, if you are making an average wage, you need two incomes, or at least one and a half, to run a household in any sort of style. This has meant a huge increase in the proportion of married women working, which must have had an effect on the supply of volunteers. On the other hand, we know that, other factors being equal, those who have jobs are more likely to take part in community activities than those who have not, and that this is as true for women as it is for men. So the increase in the proportion of women working outside the home does not necessarily mean that community-mindedness will fall.

But the form of women's engagement has changed. A working woman might coach a soccer team or join a professional association. But she will not have the time or the inclination to bake cakes or make pickles. Even the stalwarts who made the frilly coathangers seem to have gone into permanent decline.

The data show that there are plenty of people, including many men in their fifties and sixties, with time on their hands. But these people are not given to volunteering. For those prematurely on the social scrap-heap, there is not much of a sense of connectedness to build on. Others no doubt feel they 'did their bit' when the kids were younger, and are now perfectly entitled to sit around in shopping malls (the security people don't usually throw them out as they do the young ones), or to drive around Australia towing large caravans.

Heaven knows, there is enough work for them to do. Delivering meals to the housebound, running scout groups and youth clubs, coaching sports teams, collecting for charities, regenerating bushland. Parents and Citizens Associations would not knock them back, either. Perhaps the government might consider a 'work for the pension' scheme? After all, the people born in the 1930s, whom I will call Generation Y, had it much easier than those born a decade earlier. They missed the depression, were too young to serve in the war, and arrived on the labour market at its absolute zenith in the 1950s. While they paid taxes throughout their working lives, they have not contributed anything like the cost of the pensions they now enjoy. Why should mutual obligation apply only to the young?

Meanwhile, the rich continue to disappoint. It used to be thought that at some point, great wealth was accompanied by a strong desire to 'give something back' to the community, either in charitable or philanthropic donations. Unfortunately, this tendency is somewhat patchily distributed and the threshold at which great wealth is considered an embarrassment, rather than an adornment, rises by the hour. It was for these reasons, after all, that the welfare state – a form of nationalised social capital – was invented in the first place.

Now that governments are out of fashion, the idea that the well-heeled should give disproportionately to charity has undergone a revival. We feel that they should do so, but charity collectors report that they have a harder time extracting money from the wealthier suburbs than in poorer areas. This may be due to the fact that the wealthy lack charitable inclinations, but more likely it relates to a general reluctance to part with one's money. The wealthy drive a very hard bargain – presumably that is how they, or their forbears, got that way.

As company profits have increased, expectations of generosity have been transferred to business, particularly large public companies such as the banks. Everyone hates banks, but why they should have a social responsibility to keep unprofitable branches running, while supermarkets, petrol stations and department stores do not, is not immediately apparent.

The very existence of community organisations is difficult to explain in a self-interested world. From the perspective of public choice theory, it is irrational for me, and others like me, to involve ourselves in Parents and Citizens Associations. Instead, we should 'free ride' on the donated labour of others. The school fete is a compelling example: an annual event at which the parents who have done most of the work, must then spend most of the money so that other people's children reap most of the benefit. If we took the theory to its logical conclusion, everyone would make the same calculation, and there would be no altruistic behaviour at all.

Why then do people get involved? Having children is certainly a major risk factor. Someone I know threw a party when her last child left school, so thrilled was she, at last, to be out of the gravitational field of obligation. As I inspect my own motivations more deeply, I realise I must be getting some sort of personal satisfaction out of being involved, but it is difficult to know exactly what that is.

It is nice to be needed, but committee work is time-consuming and often not particularly rewarding. When money is the measure of just about everything, doing things for free seems quixotic in the extreme, especially when the duties may be far from trivial. Being 'on the committee' means assuming a measure of responsibility without being paid for it. It means being accountable, however roughly, to the membership. It also means entering a world of considerable moral ambiguity.

Community organisations are organisations in their wild form, untamed by the conventions of capitalism, sometimes showing useful characteristics but, compared with their highly-bred professional counterparts, ill-disciplined and unpredictable. When you buy someone's labour, you buy their acquiescence, if not their conformity to the culture of the organisation. When people are donating their labour, they feel freer to be themselves. Where other organisations have a culture, community organisations have a history, and often a turbulent one at that.

The nominal values of the organisation are no guide at all as to how it actually behaves. Church groups, for example, are among the most volatile of all. A friend of mind was so repulsed by the cut-throat politics on her parish council ('They left their religion at the church door,' she said) that she became a Buddhist. But the Buddhists had politics, too, complicated by the fact that there was no music to speak of and my friend was a keen chorister. When, disillusioned once again, she left, she was told it was due to her 'karma'. Oh dear.

Historical societies, perhaps because many of the members are fairly historic themselves, breed long-lived enmities. I know of one such society where the president and the secretary distrusted each other so much, they raided each other's letter boxes in order to see the information the other was getting. This had been going on for years, apparently, and everyone seemed comfortable with it. Other groups split and split again, like atoms undergoing fission, producing tiny rival entities with slightly different names, a situation guaranteed to ensure that the innocent newcomer ends up offending everyone.

Meetings of community organisations are especially problematic, because people do not feel obliged to turn up. What happens is therefore very unpredictable. If the person who always insists on formal motions and a show of hands is present, there will be formal motions and a show of hands. If not, there will be desultory discussion punctuated by 'well, what have we decided then?' Either way, the secretary writes down what he or she thinks has happened, the president goes ahead with what he or she thinks ought to have been decided, and the treasurer ignores it all, especially if spending money is involved. One secretary I know of produced such creative minutes it was difficult to get them passed. No one recognised the events she described, even if they had actually been at the meeting in question.

There are three main types of personality to be found at meetings. There is the 'Oncer'. This is the person who has a particular question, problem or grievance. They turn up once, and because regular members of the committee mistake them for a potential new member, they lavish an inordinate amount of time upon them, only to find that they never reappear.

Then there is the Livewire, the Person with Ideas. I have never understood why People with Ideas are regarded with such awe. They are, in my experience, quite plentiful. The people who are really rare are those with the persistence to carry an idea through.

The Person with Ideas goes through the average committee like a knife through butter. They have usually been on Another Committee where they ran event after event which generated thousands of dollars. Everyone was happy, pausing only in their mutual congratulation to think up yet another brilliant idea.

So the brilliant idea is unveiled – a chocolate drive; a bikathon; a bushdance. To express reservations about these ideas is to be regarded with deep distaste. 'We must encourage people like Jeff,' said our president. 'He is so enthusiastic and has so many good ideas.'

'But the last good idea, he went off overseas and dumped it on you.'

'Well, I didn't mind. At least, not that much.'

Funnily enough, a lot of Jeff's good ideas seem to involve friends and relations – the bush band turns out to be his immediate family. The cake stall is supplied by his wife's shop.

Then there is the Speechmaker. Speechmakers are usually, although not always, male, and need to hear the sound of their own voice in order to find fulfilment. Even expert chairmen can be defeated by the Speechmaker. Amateur ones search in vain for a gap in the flow. The Speechmaker usually has a French expression which, no matter what the issue under discussion, subtends the conversation with the persistence of a migraine headache.

Related to the Speechmaker is the person who 'remembers when'. Having someone who remembers when is vitally important, because the records of the community organisation have a habit of disappearing in someone's trailer to the tip. 'We tried that in 1982 and it didn't work' is valuable information. But 'that reminds me of the time Bob and Fred had a quarrel about this very thing' is not.

Communication in all organisations tends to be a hit or miss affair. In the community organisation, the conversations that actually take place never seem to be the ones that are needed. Like families, we communicate obliquely and in fragments, assuming a shared currency of meaning where none exists. When one person says they will do something, they will do it no matter what. When another says the same thing, they mean 'I will do it unless something happens which makes me change my mind'. So misunderstandings abound, compounded by the lack of formal organisation.

'I thought Fred was supposed to do that.'

'But he thought you were bringing the barbecue.'

'Has anyone seen the letter from the Jumping Castle man?'

'Where's the key?'

'Exactly who is the Public Officer this year?'

Nothing is harder than fund-raising. If you want to run a fete you have to buy things in, or obtain donations, and try to sell them at a price which will raise some money. This is fine as long as you are selling food or drink. People do not bat an eyelid at spending ten dollars on a couple of coffees and a slice of pie. But try to sell them two books for a dollar fifty and you have problems.

Let us return to my bookstall. The sun has made a fitful appearance. A former workmate, jaunty in a panama, gives me a friendly wave. 'Wouldn't catch him dead doing something like this,' I think to myself. One woman lugging a handful of paperbacks has raided her small change jar. She laboriously counts out a dollar and five cents. 'I need another forty-five cents,' I say. 'That's a dollar fifty. They'd be a bargain at twice the price. And it's for the school.'

'That's all I have,' she says. She has the books. What can I do?

Friends who ran a garage sale tell similar stories. Reluctance to pay is deeply embedded in many in our society. Economic rationalism? Tell me about it.

What are these hard-earned funds needed for? This turns out to be a very good question. Even the smallest organisation believes it must have money. If there are regular meetings, there needs to be a place to have them. Then there needs to be a newsletter. So the organisation needs money just to do nothing.

I know of some community organisations which need

money simply because the members cannot give up loss-making activities to which they are deeply attached. (It reminds me of the farmer who won the lottery. When asked what he was going to do with the money, he replied that he thought he would go on farming until it was all gone.) For the neophyte fund-raiser, there is nothing quite like the dawning realisation that, having raised the money, it is now about to be blown by someone else.

Even the most mundane activities have become enormously expensive. Kids' sports teams, which would once have been content with a few oranges at half time, now require sponsorship to keep up the supply of Gatorade. As for schools, the list of needs expands endlessly. When playgrounds were covered in asphalt and the only technology was a blackboard, schools must have been a lot less expensive to run. Now, they need landscaped grounds and labs full of computers. As the computers keep breaking down, or are trashed by their users, maintenance is a heavy ongoing expense.

Parents believe their kids will not get a job unless they are exposed to computers in school, although oddly enough no school I know of teaches the one essential computer skill — touch typing — as a compulsory subject. No one dares to question whether computer proficiency is actually necessary for a good education. Even to suggest that it might not be is to invite ridicule or, even worse, to be thought out of date. Yet computers are just another machine. We do not install dishwashers or motor cars in schools so that the children can learn how to operate them. Why computers?

The alternative to fund-raising is to get a grant. Those who are knowledgeable about such matters tell me that it is almost unknown for grants to be offered for things which actually need to be done. So it is necessary to make the real purpose look like the politically approved one. For example, if the school playground needs fixing up, there is sure to be absolutely no money available for this purpose, unless it can be shown that the playground is a safety hazard. On the other hand, there is bound to be money for 'educational innovation'. Some teachers at a school I know of managed to get some money for new seats by presenting them as an 'outdoor instructional arena'. If the playground happens to be in a marginal electorate, and there is an election in the offing, so much the better.

If the traditional community sector is eroding, the line between not-for-profit or charitable organisations and the public – or is it the private? – sector is becoming more blurred. Governments have recently discovered the potential of these third sector organisations to undertake 'service delivery', something which public servants used to do, but for which they are now considered unsuited. Volunteers would, I imagine, always have a place in these operations, but as service delivery becomes more professionalised, it is likely to be a diminishing role.

Governments will pay someone in the private sector to deliver meals on wheels, but they will not pay for the time it takes to stop and have a chat with the clients. Only the middle-aged to elderly ladies who give their time for nothing will do that. How long will they keep doing it? My guess is that my generation, the baby boomers, will not view their social obligations in the same way. They will reason that, if the givers are on the decline, the only way to deal with the takers is by making them, or their families, pay. The same logic will certainly be visited upon us, in our turn, by the vengeful members of generation X, who have reportedly never forgiven us for not only living through the 1970s, but for talking about it so much.

If all the people who do things for others out of charity or duty were suddenly to stop doing so, would our society collapse? Would the person who says 'I really admire what you're doing', but never offers to help, suddenly do their share? Or would public funds somehow be found? Perhaps Nellie Melba had the right idea. She gave many concerts for good causes, but objected to the widespread assumption that she was always available to knock out a song for free. At one soiree, the hostess was particularly importunate. 'Surely,' she cried, 'it is no trouble to sing a little song.'

'Surely,' the diva replied with characteristic bluntness, 'it is no trouble to write a little cheque.'

CONFESSIONS OF A BUSH TREASURER

Contrary to our imagined reputation for hell-raising, we Aussies are natural bureaucrats. Put three of us together, and we have a president, a secretary and a treasurer in no time. The president is usually the most gregarious, and sees herself making speeches, the secretary thinks 'writing the minutes won't be too much trouble', and whoever is left over becomes treasurer.

No one ever wants to be treasurer. Even in government, where ministerial posts are everything, being treasurer is considered the hardest job, tolerated by the ambitious only as a stepping-stone to the sunny uplands of the prime ministership.

I had never even thought of being treasurer until, unable to bear the silence at an annual general meeting, I volunteered for the job. Innocent of any book-keeping or accounting knowledge, I embarked on my career as a bush treasurer. (A bush treasurer is a bit like a bush lawyer – more arse than class.)

Unlike the political treasurer, treasurers in small organisations are involved in handling money, banking it, recording it, wondering either where it went or what to do with it. And anything involved in Handling Money attracts fear and loathing. Money is where the promises stop and the reality begins.

Treasurers are not required to generate money, thank goodness. But they are required to be accountable for it. Accountability, like most character-building processes, is always more bracing when applied to other people. Undergoing it oneself can be a distinctly uncomfortable experience. How to explain what looks like a meagre achievement when doing anything at all represented a significant victory over the ever-present forces of inertia? How to justify a decision which, given the advantages of hindsight, one would never have made? How to give, to someone who has not experienced them, the flavour of opposing personalities and points of view, all the dreary accommodations and negotiations of organisational life?

A business needs to earn money to keep going. Public and not-for-profit organisations face a different set of problems. There seem to be only two types of organisation – those with more money than they can sensibly spend, and those with no money at all. Of the two, the first is probably more difficult to manage, because there is a suspicion that any surpluses have been gouged from the pockets of the poor or at least the unsuspecting. The second unites everyone in the inevitability of decline from which any respite no matter how small is greeted with jubilation.

Just as individuals and even nations are said to have financial personalities, so do organisations. Undoubtedly the worst organisation of which I was treasurer was a creche catering to the needs of the children of academics. No one had any skills whatsoever, but the committee was hellbent on spending any semblance of a surplus. It was in vain that I lectured them about cash flow. By contrast, another voluntary organisation had surpluses stashed away which might have interested Kerry Packer, for gambling money at any rate. This organisation had a very different personality – the money was for 'contingencies' but what they were, or when they might eventuate, was never discussed.

Some organisations startle at the merest mention of fiscal difficulty. Others positively enjoy it. One society I am acquainted with had a cash flow crisis at the end of every year. It was such a regular occurrence, people even looked forward to it. The reason was perfectly obvious – it received most of its income at the beginning of the year, and had a regular pattern of expenditure. There was another problem – income and expenditure did not quite balance. The problem could have been remedied, but that would have required planning, and various kinds of economies. It would also have deprived everyone of the gratifying frisson of wondering whether this year was the one that would finally, irretrievably, bring the society to an end.

The treasurer is the one person who gets criticised in voluntary organisations. I think this is because people expect money questions to be straightforward. In practice, they rarely are. Assuming that the banking is being done, and the paperwork is not simply being stuffed into a shoe box, everything else, even in the simplest organisation, is interpretation. Financial management is as much about 'gut feel' as it is about numbers. The numbers do not yield their meaning readily. Indeed in many ways, they have no meaning at all, except in a comparative sense.

Accounting is usually described as bean-counting, yet it could just as easily be termed the epistemology of money. Imperfect as it is as a measure, it is the only one which unites apples and oranges, stocks and flows, buildings and Bollinger in a common calculus. Money, in itself, gives no hint of where it has been. 'Money has no smell,' the emperor Vespasian is said to have observed when a member of his entourage remonstrated with him for placing a tax on toilets.

A balance sheet is like a photograph, a moment in time, when hundreds of different processes are temporarily, arbitrarily, stopped in their tracks, and we are confronted with the trace they leave on our financial receptors. What has happened is a matter of history, and what is about to happen, of conjecture. The camera which takes the photograph is highly selective. It sees the assets and the liabilities, but not the people or the problems.

It is not true that accounting is as dry as dust. Shakespeare had a taste for business, if not for accounting, and business terms often crop up in his plays and poetry, as if their very precision appealed to him as a way of describing emotional ideas. What about 'summer's lease hath all too short a date' which ends the first quatrain of Sonnet 18 ('Shall I compare thee to a summer's day')? Or, the last two lines of Sonnet 30, which refer to the 'sad account of fore-bemoaned moan, which I now pay as if not paid before?' And who can forget how the great American writer Edith Wharton once described marriage as 'the slow lifelong acquittal of a debt contracted in ignorance'?

The bush treasurer learns quickly that, while transparency is all very well, it is a mistake to reveal too much. Sometimes people simply don't want to know what is going on, because the reality is too depressing. Even if the society or organisation is going broke, in fact especially if it is, people will find ways of not discussing it, while seizing on minor details. Focusing attention where and when it is needed is not easy.

Then again, if too many people know what is going on, disputes can become even more virulent than when they were based on guesswork. When one university I know of tried to establish clearer criteria for allocating resources, there were far more fights than there had been before, because the intricate web of cross subsidies that had sustained the place was gradually exposed to view. Far from welcoming this illumination, those who were subsidising the others felt even more aggrieved than before, and those who were being subsidised felt even less appreciated than before. The status quo is not just an equilibrium of sorts, it is a moral artefact, another reason why it is so difficult to bring about change.

Of course, the treasurer may have no more idea about what is going on than anyone else. He or she must pretend to omniscience. But even in the simplest organisation, strange things can happen. An innocuous decision may turn out to have all sorts of unexpected consequences. Or there may be surprises lurking in the balance sheet.

One treasurer told me about an awful sinking feeling when he realised that an amount which had been included for years in the accounts as an asset was actually money 'parked' by someone years ago which did not belong to the organisation at all. The insurance company HIH found itself in possession of a less innocent legacy when it bought FAI Insurance and discovered that the assets were actually poised over a black hole of soon-to-be-realised losses. But in my experience, bush treasurers at least try to get it right, in contrast to at least some of the professionals. As Ansett Airlines, then one of Australia's best-known companies, slid inexorably into insolvency, no one, apparently, was even minding the shop.

Professional skills may even make things worse. An Anglican minister told me what happened when a qualified accountant became the Hon. Treasurer of the parish. 'It was all fairly simple up to that point,' he lamented. 'There was the collection plate and my salary, the maintenance and the overhead [this turned out to be the bishop]. But the accountant brought in a new information system which nobody else could understand. When he left, we had to start all over again.'

The advent of the GST added a whole new dimension to being treasurer. The tax office saved some of its finest performances for not-for-profit organisations. I'll never forget the meeting at which two tax office representatives disagreed with each other about the circumstances under which certain kinds of organisations had to register for GST. Finally someone in the audience got up and said, 'If you two guys can't agree, what on earth are we supposed to do?'

'It's all very complicated,' one of the officials replied.

What sort of financial personality should the bush treasurer adopt? There is a temptation to be stern and somewhat scrooge-like, a grim parent to the laughing kiddies. Most people love to socialise, so every occasion, no matter how trivial, must be accompanied by the serving of food and drink. Deeply unpopular is the treasurer who points out that the populace is, by and large, well enough fed not to need it. There is also an invariable rule which states that, no matter how many people you cater for, it will always be too much or too little.

There is something deep in the human psyche which does not like the process of budgeting. For one thing, it involves weighing the benefits of one decision against those of another. We don't like doing this because our preferences are often emotionally based. Even worse, it means extending this activity into the future, which no one likes to do, because it involves a lot of work, and you might change your mind, anyway. So urgent requests 'come up' throughout the year.

To set priorities in a budget round is to confront the awful matter of trade-offs. 'Can we afford it?' the question that is the bane of every bush treasurer's existence means asking 'how much value do we attach to the next best purchase we might think of making with the money?' This is such an awful question that we compartmentalise things as much as possible to avoid having to answer it. So every bit of the organisation has its own budget, and everyone gets a bit more (or a bit less) than last year. Unless they make a fuss, of course. Or it's their 'turn'.

Next to consider is the fungibility principle (not to be confused with mushrooms), a vital concept when, as many not-for-profits do, you are raising money for other people to spend. Money is like water – unless it's dammed and walled off, it substitutes readily for other bits of money. So if you're giving someone money, and you want to be sure you are making a difference, how do you satisfy yourself that you are not simply saving the organisation funds it would have spent anyway? Like the Commonwealth with its specific purpose payments to the states, it is difficult for the funder to be sure, unless the fundee is prepared to be unusually open. Then again, if the organisation you are supporting grows to rely on your funds, what incentives does it have to use its resources wisely? Helpers everywhere have the same, nagging, doubt – are the recipients doing their bit, too?

Running small organisations really concentrates the mind because if you get it wrong, the consequences of your own actions are real and immediate. Large organisations are constructed to fracture and dilute accountability. In small ones, the chill drafts blow around your neck the whole time. You never know what is going to happen next, partly because the consequences of your own actions are hard to predict, and partly because the aftermath of decisions taken long ago, by other people, can come back to haunt you. Incorporation protects against individual liability, and insurance handles the rest, or so we like to think. But the stress when something goes wrong can be considerable. A friend who was treasurer of a ski club which lost its entire ski lodge found himself in a free-for-all of people suing each other after the disastrous landslide at Thredbo in the Snowy Mountains in 1997.

One of the hardest things is employing people. Small employers are really at the mercy of the market. If they don't have a reliable network to use, the information asymmetry is huge. And then if you make a mistake, you cannot get rid of the person without running the risk of unfair dismissal proceedings. Contrary to the rhetoric of the Human Resource Industry there are only two kinds of employee – those who can do the job, and those who can't. If you have inherited or recruited one of the latter, you are in for a hard time.

Everyone has stories to tell. Restaurant owners are particularly vulnerable to drunken chefs who terrorise the staff and, on occasion, the customers as well. Good chefs are hard to come by, so their eccentricities are usually tolerated unless it turns out that they cannot cook either, in which case all is lost unless they leave voluntarily. Under Unfair Dismissal laws, an employee has to be literally falling down drunk on the job before an employer can get rid of him or her without an elaborate procedure of documented failings and warnings.

My story is about Theodora, the lady who ran the school uniform shop. Theodora was a spectacular-looking woman of vaguely Mediterranean background, with flashing dark eyes and hair that had gone prematurely white – a result, she told me, of her husband going broke on account of the introduction of a GST in Canada. Why, she railed, did we have to do it in Australia? A good point.

It was always instructive to visit the bank with Theodora. She swept through the door, scattering queues before her. She did not believe in waiting, but would simply walk up to the nearest teller, leaving the person at the head of the queue gaping in amazement. The tellers, particularly the male ones, would jump to do her bidding. At first, being like most Anglos genetically programmed to join queues, I was full of admiration. 'How did you do that?' I asked. 'They were just people waiting,' she replied, 'we had business to perform.'

Theodora loved running the shop, but her management style was somewhat idiosyncratic. She took to railing against children, even quite small ones, who were not wearing what she regarded as the school uniform. There were complaints about these sometimes tearful encounters. But Theodora was quite unabashed. Why, she asked, have a uniform shop when the school could not enforce the wearing of uniforms anyway? Another good point.

Theodora continued to do things her way. She bullied volunteers into running the shop for her while she went off to attend to her own affairs. She forgot to write out receipts, so that there was always more money in the bank than could be accounted for. She regarded this as something to be proud of, telling me things would be much worse if there was less money than there should be. Another good point?

Theodora was not so much economical with the truth, as oblivious of it. She could claim black was white, and truly believe it. She was also a past master of the art of diversion. You might recall that Mr Dick in *David Copperfield*, no matter how the conversation had started, always ended up talking about King Charles's head. Well, Theodora was the opposite. The conversation would start out clearly focused on some management matter, but would then, suddenly and mysteriously, turn into melodrama.

If I complained that the cash book was not properly written up, she would launch into a tirade about the slackness of various suppliers. If the shop's opening hours changed from week to week without warning, she would talk about the perfidy of people in general, and the lack of flexibility which led them to expect regular opening hours.

Finally, the day came when the shop did not open at all. I said I thought we had come to the end of the road, and she agreed. 'You should resign,' she said. With great difficulty, I convinced her that it was she who should go. Theodora extracted a reference from me, which I produced with gritted teeth, hoping that any prospective employer would understand the coded messages embedded within it. I was feeling quite pleased with myself when, with a sickening lurch, I realised that I would have to find someone to replace her.

As a neophyte in someone else's world, the bush treasurer

soon discovers that whatever questions she has, she can never put them in a form to which it is possible to obtain straight answers. The realisation dawns that the professionals, the accountants and auditors, are not there to help you manage the organisation. They are there to satisfy the regulators, the bureaucrats. The bureaucrats, as we know, are there to administer the law, which in most matters has long since lost touch with reality.

Take the annual audit. Most small organisations have very basic records, and cannot afford to produce financial statements which are then checked by the auditor. So the auditor prepares the accounts, and then audits his own handiwork. Of course, checks are run on the basic cash records, on the assumption that the treasurer has, or wants to, run off to South America with the cake stall proceeds.

But there are traps here. For some reason, inter-year comparability and comprehensible figures do not go together. Thus you can have the same categories of expenditure year after year, but no one on the committee has any idea what they mean. Alternatively, you can get the categories changed so that they mean something, but then, inevitably, alarmist members of the committee demand to know why something has gone from zero last year to thousands this year.

Auditors are strange beings. Having seen them at work, it is no wonder they get things wrong when they sign off on accounts. They run tests to see whether the organisation's records are reliable. But they are simply comparing one part of the system with another. An organisation with things to hide can make sure the records match up – it's just they don't give a true picture of what is really happening.

My own experience is that the more records you keep, the more likely it is that there will be a mistake, and something doesn't add up to the right amount. For the honest organisation, this leads to more trouble and expense sorting things out. For the dishonest one, the sky is the limit. One organisation in the public sector kept so few records, when the time came for the auditor to do his job, there was nothing to work with, so he could not give it a bad audit report.

To be fair, voluntary organisations must make accountants tear their hair. Decisions are made with no real thought for the consequences. A child care centre I was associated with spent thousands of dollars on an extension. The only problem was, it did not own the building it had extended. The extension was listed as an asset in the accounts, but if the society were wound up, there was no way its value could be realised. When I pointed this out to the auditor, he agreed that this was a problem, and muttered something about 'negative equity'. I never did find out what this mind-blowing concept actually meant.

The culmination of the treasurer's year is the annual general meeting. AGMs come in two types: those where hardly anyone turns up, and those where half the country seems to turn up. The bush treasurer pretends to be pleased when the latter occurs, but inwardly he or she is seething. Most sane people avoid AGMs like the plague, so attendance may not necessarily augur well. Paranoia creeps in. Are these people really entitled to be here? Why do some of them show such an unhealthy interest in the financial statements? A large attendance does not necessarily mean a flow of volunteers for the committee positions, but possibly an imminent mugging for the incumbents.

After the AGM comes the reporting to the authorities and the lodgment of the forms. State government authorities are very conservative institutions, so even in these days of e-government, and talk of customer service, they still go out of their way to make the lodgment of forms for incorporated entities as character-building an exercise as possible.

Firstly, the forms require lots of signatures, so that whoever is coordinating the job has to remember to bring them to the AGM. Secondly, the forms follow the law of inverse space. Pioneered by US Customs and Immigration, this law requires that the longer the answer to a question is likely to be, the less room you allow for its transmission, and vice versa. Thirdly, all forms must have a box headed 'Registration number', with little demarcations within it suggesting a prescribed number of digits, but no suggestion as to what the number actually is. This drives tidy-minded people absolutely wild. Fourthly, if there are any simpler bits that the person filling in the form might be able to understand, these are placed in a section surrounded by a strongly-marked border and headed 'Staff use only'. Finally, forms stipulate ferocious penalties for late lodgment. This ensures that organisations that never get around to lodging their form, or are too demoralised to fill it in, get off scot-free, while those who do the right thing although a bit late, get it in the neck.

Having filled in the form, you must then find the place to lodge it. Most agencies try to make this a challenging experience by requiring you to find a subterranean office indicated by the most discreet or cryptic of signs, staffed by a large number of persons, none of whom turns out to be equipped to receive your form. Then, when the right person finally appears, she bangs a whacking great stamp on the thing and puts it in a tray. 'Don't you need to check it?' I asked one year. She gave me a steely stare. 'We'll be in touch,' she said, 'if there is anything wrong.' But I am sure nobody ever looked at it again.

Being treasurer is not really a job for wimps. Every AGM, you resolve that this is positively, finally, the last year you will do it. But then, something almost proprietorial sneaks in. No one else understands it as well as you do. What if your successor loses the well-maintained files (the last lot somehow got taken to the tip), or fails to understand the beauty of the GST set-up?

The ultimate bush treasurer, Paul Keating, seemed to feel this way. According to his biographer John Edwards, after a few years in the job Keating believed he understood 'how all the levers worked'. Driving the economy was a bit like driving a steam engine—throttle, brakes, Paris option. That was in the early days, though, before the economy either wouldn't start or, having started, couldn't be stopped. Then it went off the rails completely, doing permanent damage to the engine driver's reputation.

Even before then, I can imagine how Keating started to chafe against the limitations of the treasurer's role. It's dreary. You're taken for granted. There are things that are worrying. You have responsibility, but no real power. The top job beckons—surely it is time you presided, rather than adopting the functionary's role. Keating overturned the incumbent, but he was much less successful in the job than his predecessor, Bob Hawke, had been. Sometimes, you just have to know your own limitations.

DO YOU MIND?

Quiet, please. I am trying to meditate. I am sitting cross-legged on the floor, because this is what I have been advised to do. The body forms a stable triangle in this position. But it hurts.

Almost anything is more interesting than meditation. Duties that are normally shoved to the back of one's mind assume a new and diverting urgency – constructing shopping lists, cleaning the mould off the grouting in the shower, making postponed telephone calls. One doesn't actually do them, of course, one just thinks about doing them. This is called distraction.

The meditating figure has an irresistible fascination to any children who happen to be in the vicinity. They appear, sighing and big-eyed. A major school project they have forgotten to tell you about is due in *today*. Their sports uniform cannot be found. This, too, is called distraction.

Many people claim to meditate regularly, but I think it just feels as though they are. Those who take to it readily can, in fact, be off-putting up close. I remember a couple who told me they meditated together for 45 minutes every morning. (There was no mention of children, so I could well believe it.) They were both possessed of a somewhat chilling calm, and seemed to look down upon the world from a great height.

I wondered what they had been like before they started meditating. Perhaps they had been bug-eyed with frenzy. Somehow I did not think so. The problem for the rest of us is that meditation does not turn meditators into better people. Whatever it is they discover on their inward journey does not produce greater warmth, or consideration for others, merely an unnerving composure.

Most of us don't know what to do with our minds, most of the time. They do our bidding well enough when we have a job to do, and they generally find the right things to say on social occasions.

But give them a chink of opportunity and they fill it with aimless chatter, memories, resentments. Our bodies know immediately what is 'not us'. But our minds – well, they have a mind of their own.

Traditions of mind training still have a place in Eastern philosophies. In the West, they have all but died out, as monastic religion has declined and decayed. Institutional religion, whether of the jump and holler or High Church variety, offers little in the way of usable spiritual technologies, leaving many people the task of finding (or forging) their own. Every so often, we hear of a pop star who has embraced transcendental meditation or scientology. We tell ourselves there is something missing from our lives without ever quite working out what it is.

We have amusement and entertainment industries of vast proportions to fill in the gaps. Sports events are filled with amplified cacophony. Lifts and shopping malls trail little threads of music. Long-distance bus drivers play the radio all the time. Runners clamp themselves into a pair of headphones. Picnics are incomplete without the ghetto blaster. Anything, it seems, rather than the sound of silence.

Even our fantasies are pre-packaged for us, by some of the strangest people on the planet. Are we all as interested in compulsive sex and mindless violence as many contemporary film directors? I suspect not—many of us prefer them the other way around—but we are persuaded by the apparent interest of others that we ought to pay attention. Minds have a bit of the herd instinct about them. They do not like being alone.

The paradox, of course, is that it takes a mind to know a mind. When we think of ourselves 'from the outside' we exhaust ourselves trying to come up with suitable images for the brain—a system, a structure, a biochemical hive, a piece of software. When we attempt to know our minds 'from the inside' we quickly run up against the limits of introspection. There is so much of our minds that we can never know, yet the parts that we don't understand are a substantial part of who we are. Even the conscious apparatus of thinking and feeling—the subject matter of cognitive science and of psychology—is accessible to us as its owners only through the uncertain light of reflection.

At birth, we are each presented with this amazing machine, with no operating instructions. How do we work out what kind of mind we have? How do we decide whether we are smart or dumb, practical or theoretical, logical or intuitive? There are psychological tests which purport to tell us, but for most people the choices begin to be made much earlier on, in the giant sorting machine called school.

For a brief time, there are dreams. We learn of the great minds of the past, and wonder whether we might think of joining them on their quest. For a brief time, the ideas really matter. Then, as Bernard Shaw put it, our education begins to be interrupted by our schooling.

Kids who are smart realise early on that they learn faster than others. If they are really smart they learn to disguise it. In a country which still has a good deal of the crudeness of the frontier about it, it does not pay to be too clever. I often wonder why we set such store on artificial intelligence, when we waste so much of the natural variety.

Parents are convinced that good teaching makes all the difference to their kids. Every teacher knows that beyond a certain point, everything depends upon aptitude, interest and home support. Intellectual growth is hard to predict. I had a schoolteacher who used to talk about the size of people's minds. Some minds, she explained, grew and grew. Others stayed pretty much as they were. But it was difficult to tell which was going to be which.

Minds have relative, as well as absolute, sizes: as the competition intensifies, they seem to shrink. What seemed a great talent at school may fade in comparison with the best at university, or in the workplace. Changing tack may change the equation, though. Jeff Bezos, the founder of Amazon.com, discovered when he reached Princeton that he could only ever be a mediocre theoretical physicist. But he became a first-rate entrepreneur.

For many kids, school is a sort of code which they never learn to crack. I had a student who put in an essay which was complete gobbledegook. At that stage, I believed that it made sense to try to teach people how to write better essays. In reality, most people do not really care about how well or otherwise they write. Some can be taught to improve by coaching, but it is debatable how deep-seated the effect is.

But sometimes there is a breakthrough. I observed to the student who had submitted the gobbledegook that when we talk about the world, we normally expect to understand what we say. An essay, I explained, is not an exercise in putting words together in some weird kind of pattern. It is an act of communication. Any idea can be put simply. I saw comprehension dawning. It was as though I had liberated her from a prison. I don't recall that her revised draft was enormously improved, but at least she had grasped the idea that if it did not make sense to her, it probably did not make sense to anyone else either.

Even the best minds do not function well without constant stimulation. 'I haven't read a book in years,' said a former school friend re-met by chance. I didn't tell her that it showed. After the weather, and the friends remembered, there is not much to sustain a dialogue without some sort of reference to the world of words.

The spoken word beguiles us, because we can capture so much of it electronically. But how much of it shrivels and dies when it is written down! Even good conversation is difficult to sustain without reading because without it, thoughts and opinions are endlessly recycled, a bit like talkback radio. Reading requires concentration, and generally we will not invest the necessary energy and attention unless the mind so encountered is worth the effort.

Thanks to semiotics, we can understand much more of the collective mind than we used to. The way people prune trees, or design margarine tubs can be deeply revealing. But reading is language, and language is understanding.

When travelling recently in Turkey, we could see and speak and observe. We even mastered a few words of the language. But we could not begin to understand because we could not read. In France, on the other hand, we could read enough of the daily newspapers to understand a good deal more of what was going on, and even something of how it felt. It was the time mad cow disease was first officially acknowledged in France. 'Plus qu'on sait, plus qu'on a peur', wrote a columnist in *Le Figaro* – the more one knows, the more one is afraid. Precisely.

For any given level of intelligence, there are many different kinds of minds. There are people who have minds like meat cleavers, and who chop problems up into pieces. They succeed in the law, which is one reason why legal decisions are so often reversed on appeal. It is because the meat-cleaver mind chops the problem up in different ways at different times.

Then there are the classifiers, those who know where everything fits (very common in academia). Are you talking about X or about Y? they will ask. The classifiers like things to be neat and tidy and are often venomous about any kind of intellectual creativity.

Connectors, or systems thinkers, do not get on well with classifiers. There is an anecdote in James Gleick's biography of the American physicist Richard Feynman, who was once mocked by a fellow student because he did not know that a particular bird was called a brown-throated thrush.

Feynman recalled what his father had told him. 'You can know the name of a bird in all the languages of the world, but when you're finished, you'll know absolutely nothing whatever about the bird. You'll only know about humans in different places and what they call the bird. So let's look at the bird and see what it's doing – that's what counts.'

But understanding what the bird is doing means understanding the world in which it lives. And that is a great deal more work than simply giving it a label.

The synthesiser is probably the most interesting of all. Synthesisers do not know what they are not supposed to know and can therefore come up with new ways of looking at a problem. Watson and Crick, who worked out the shape of the double helix, needed to bring together insights from a number of disciplines, some of which they knew very little about. But they were prepared to ask the right dumb questions.

Then there are styles of thinking. Some people are happy with equations. Others prefer diagrams. The economist Max Corden worked out ways of illustrating incredibly complex propositions in welfare economics by drawing diagrams of them. My father always asked for 'thinking paper' when we asked him to explain something. He would draw lines, arrows, boxes. Sometimes we could follow them, sometimes not. But it is only when we explain something to ourselves that we have a basis for explaining it to someone else.

Most mysterious of all is imagination – rich, elusive, indispensable. It pops up in the unexpected verbal flourish, in the way a friend decorates her house, in a story told in a certain way. Capitalism pretends to be about knowledge and money, but it is really imagination which it craves, manipulates and ultimately destroys.

There are other attributes of mind, of course. Some people like to control the world through plans. Others are so laid back, it is a wonder they can stand up. They never plan anything in advance, but leave things to the ebb and flow of fate. They are relaxed about uncertainty.

Then there are people who take stands on matters of principle. My grandfather would never buy Arab dates, because of the Arabs' attitudes to Israel. The date scones he began making when my grandmother died had to contain Californian dates, even though Californian dates were often difficult to come by. He also refused to set foot in Paris, because of de Gaulle's lack of gratitude after the war. The General may or may not have been put out by my grandfather's non-arrival, but that was not the point. My grandfather, at least, had made his.

I have noticed that left-leaning people try particularly hard to protect themselves from moral contamination. The late Judith Wright would never knowingly read anything which contained the wrong political attitudes. She would not read the *Australian* because it was published by Rupert Murdoch. As for *Quadrant*, it was completely beyond the pale. I know many other people who will not read *Quadrant*, not because they might not enjoy it, but because they are expected to disapprove of it.

Maintaining principles can get very confusing. We had a

bit of a boycott on Australian-owned Arnotts biscuits after the company was taken over by American conglomerate Campbells, but after a while, we forgot about it. It's so difficult to maintain concentration in the supermarket. I suppose this is what is meant by globalisation.

There are also people who get offended by things. Unlike those who avoid ideas they don't like, those who take offence are constantly on the lookout for provocations that will get them going. They go to art galleries they know will have carefully crafted outrages that are bound to offend them. Then they get offended, and complain.

Once I published a short story in a journal I was editing. It was a very good short story about two boys who, for reasons they scarcely understand, career around a country town dragging a live sheep behind their ute. The story did not condone this sort of thing, of course. It was about understanding what leads to it.

But someone wrote in who was Offended. Why, I wondered, had this person deliberately bought an obscure, self-styled radical publication when it was almost certain to contain something offensive? (Indeed its publishers would have been mortified if it had not.) Why could she not have taken a stand instead, and not bought the thing in the first place?

Politically correct people get offended a lot, too, not because they enjoy being offended, but because they have a knack of finding offence in unexpected places. For example, there was someone on the radio the other day who was offended by a Tim Tam ad which referred to afternoon tea as 'secret women's business'.

I suppose that underneath, it is about being righteous. The Bible is full of references to righteous men and, occasionally, women. Jesus himself, if I remember correctly, was not big on righteousness. But the powerbrokers most certainly were. Righteousness has always been much more highly regarded than being good, partly because its effects are much less unsettling, and also because it is much easier to measure against performance indicators. You know the sort of thing: mantras recited; rosaries told; dollars handed over.

None of us knows what will happen to our minds as we age. Will we lose the proverbial marbles, or move majestically into an era of higher-order sagacity? More to the point, who will be around to lament the first or marvel at the second? Will they (or we) be able to tell the difference?

Minds are not just unruly, catching trains of thought to unexpected destinations. Sometimes they go off the rails all together. For a society which values predictability, conformity and success more than ever before, mental illness poses signal problems for the building of the CV, or resume as I believe it is now called.

There are special Olympic games for the physically and intellectually disabled and they have, quite rightly, insisted on a place at our common table. But there are no parades of mental illness pride, no marches of schizophrenics down Oxford Street. Those who get over it, learn to hide it.

All illnesses are constructs to some extent, but with mental illness, we are on particularly difficult ground. If normality is a consensus, being mentally ill is an experience of being judged.

Foucault, who wrote tellingly on these matters, considered insanity to be an invention of the nineteenth century, when the insane began to be locked away on a systematic basis. Before then, madness, or the force of unreason, could afflict anyone at any time. It was not something which was believed to come from within the individual. Mad people were possessed by forces external to themselves.

But once 'madness' changed from the primeval force of unreason into an identifiable human form, the psyche began to be personalised in a way which was new. In inventing the concept of neurosis, Freud revealed the mind as a clever dissimulator which, given an appropriate level of insight, could be stripped of its pretences.

Every era has its favourite abnormalities. In Freud's time it was hysteria. In our own, it is depression, a polymorphous condition said to be spreading in epidemic form. Sales of anti-depressants boom. Even governments announce that More needs to be done.

Depression is clearly a mood disorder, but beyond that, nobody quite knows what it is. When men in suits run off with their secretaries and ascribe the impulse to 'depression', it is clear that we need another word for the real thing.

Dorothy Rowe calls depression 'the disease of loss'. I can think of no better way to describe it. That is what it feels like. You lose energy, connection, focus, sometimes even thought itself.

Then there is something else, something it is almost impossible to describe. Even a fine writer like William Styron could get nowhere near it. A sort of dread. A consciousness of darkness so close you can almost touch it. The problem is, you can't write about it when you're experiencing it, and when you can, at last, write, you have forgotten what it was like.

We know that women become depressed more than men do, and that there are connections between depression and the flux and flow of female hormones. But nobody knows quite how it all works, and as always with human beings, social and psychological factors complicate the picture.

Is depression more common than it used to be? It may be that our intensely garrulous age just talks about it more. On the other hand, every age creates its own version of what it is to be normal. Religious mania, for example, crops up less frequently than in the past, because in general religion has lost its hold on most people's psyche.

Technology has made a difference, too, particularly to

women's lives. The physical drudgery of 50 years ago (washing nappies in a copper!) has been replaced by the chore of ferrying kids about in the car. We have energy on demand, water on tap and information on line. Most people, at least those in advanced industrial countries, report that they are pretty happy most of the time. It's just that, as we get richer, it takes more money to reach the same level of happiness.

Where, then, does depression come from? A lot of it is undoubtedly repressed anger. The cult of fame means that many people are obsessed with 'making it'. It is no longer enough to make a home, bring up the kids, and refrain from kicking the cat too often. It is necessary to be successful. But when success eludes us, or sometimes even when it does not, resentment festers, and anger flares.

If jealousy sneaks up on you like badly folded sheets pushed to the back of the shelf, anger is the carelessly stowed suitcase that falls on your head when you open the door. It is immediate, sometimes crushing. We do not know what to do with it. We are told not to suppress it, lest we develop a host of complicated illnesses, from cancer to lumbago. But expressing it is not much chop either, when it is necessary to continue to work with the person who is the object of our anger.

Are mental problems physical, psychological or both? If the brain does not function properly, behaviour and thinking are clearly impaired. But the reverse is not necessarily true – the agony of schizophrenia does not seem to be associated with any identifiable changes in the brain.

Perhaps it is the question, with its underlying Cartesian assumptions, that is the problem. The psychological may, for example, simply be the obverse side of the physical. Or the categories themselves may be just different ways of describing the same thing, artefacts of our way of thinking rather than an objective reality. Yet we long, for some reason, to believe that physical diseases are really psychological, or at least have a substantial psychological component, and psychological ones are really physical.

In both cases, the reason has to do with control. We feel stronger in the face of physical disease if we believe that meditation, or a positive attitude, can help us. At the same time, a physical cause for mental illness lets us off the hook, as well as enabling drug companies to make lots of money from anti-depressants.

While some people no doubt amble through life, wondering what all the fuss is about, the human condition is not exactly conducive to balanced happiness. As G.K. Chesterton wrote: 'In a real sense it is unnatural to be human. Either a divine being fell, or one of the animals went completely off its head.'

Most of us recognise that the differences between ourselves and those who are considered mad are differences of degree rather than of kind. We acknowledge the enormous importance of staying linked to other people in maintaining our sanity. Work is important for this reason, too. Every person has immense potential for unhappiness which must be crowded out through activity.

I notice that modern techniques for treatment are more no-nonsense than they used to be. You change your thoughts, you change the reality that underlies your thoughts. As R.D. Laing said to one of his patients who complained of hearing voices: 'Do you have to listen to them?'

The brilliant American mathematician John Nash, who spent 30 years in a schizophrenic black hole, explained that he paid attention to his weird ideas because they came from the same part of his mind as his mathematical insights. He was able to help himself get better by paying no attention to any thought that had anything to do with politics, religion or teaching. Enough said.

Sometimes even misery has a therapeutic purpose. As Woody Allen observed in *Crimes and Misdemeanours*, no one ever committed suicide in Brooklyn – they were all far too unhappy. For what I imagine are related reasons, no one ever committed suicide in wartime. Why kill yourself when someone else may do it for you at any moment?

How much choice is there in madness? The psychotherapist Dorothy Rowe is convinced that mental illness is one adaptation among many to the problem of being. It is just more dysfunctional than other choices. For some, madness has a peculiar allure. Timothy Leary deliberately pushed against the boundaries of reason in order to find liberation. It is said that the philosopher Nietzsche, who considered rationalism to be debilitating, sent himself mad as a way of living his own philosophy.

So how do you manage your mind? It turns out that the answers have been known for a very long time. In fact, we can trace a straight line from the Buddha to Jesus Christ to Marcus Aurelius to Dale Carnegie. The message is not so much about the mind, or at least the intellectual bits of it, as about the emotions. The emotions are not separate from the mind, but are created by it, and dependent upon it.

We create our own reality, in other words. This perception gives rise to practical stratagems for dealing with life's disappointments. Plutarch, who greatly admired the Stoics, tells an interesting anecdote about one Aristippus, a rich man who had unfortunately lost a good part of his estate. A sham friend commiserated with him. Aristippus was apparently not one of those people who thinks of the perfect rejoinder while catching the chariot to work the following day. 'I have three farms left, while you have only a plot of ground, I believe?' he told the sympathiser. When his interlocutor agreed, he said, 'Then should I not rather condole with you?'

Our ways of thinking are more grounded in our emotions

than most of us would care to admit. Whether one is an economic rationalist or not seems to me to have more to do with temperament than with intellectual conviction based on analysis. And every scientist knows that the biggest threat to truth is to become emotionally attached to a good idea.

We are dreadful at assessing risks sensibly, and luck is the one goddess we all worship. Maniacal drivers dangle charms from the rear view mirror, and there are many streets with no number 13. My local shopping centre has lost its only green-grocer (a victim of predatory supermarket pricing), but the feng shui man is going strong.

How credulous we are! The physicist Carl Sagan said that he always tried to be super-sceptical when someone was telling him something he really wanted to believe, but for many of us these are exactly the things we do believe.

For this reason, it is very easy to induce superstitious thinking in experimental subjects. Put the subject in a room with a machine which sometimes gives forth money, and sometimes nothing. Make the order in which this happens completely random. There is nothing the subject can do to influence the machine.

Most people decide that nothing they can do will make any difference, and sit in the corner, waiting to be let out. But a minority decides there has to be a connection, an order to the situation, and they try anything to crack the code. In one case, a young girl found that on one occasion, the money had issued forth when she raised one arm above her shoulder. She decided that she had cracked the magic formula, and spent lengthy periods of time walking around the room, periodically raising her arm, convinced that she would produce the desired result. Even when nothing happened, it did nothing to dissuade her. She remembered the first time. Instant superstitious thinking.

But before you dismiss this episode too readily, consider

this. Some years ago, when five dollars was worth a good deal more than it is today, I discovered a five dollar note in a bus shelter. The note had been pinned to the wall of the bus shelter with a message that said: 'This five dollars is cursed.' Judging by its appearance the money had obviously been there for some time. I thought about it, but couldn't bring myself to pick it up. Would you?

The future scares us much more than the past, because at least in the past, we know what happens. But that, for many of us, is precisely the problem. That leaves the present, but no less an authority than Dr Johnson said that the present was bearable only when drunk.

Ultimately, our minds are unknowable, and it is the act of communication which is all that matters. Here, too, we miss the mark more than we hit it. When I was a kid, my sister and I tried very hard to imagine what it was like being the other person. But we always gave up. How could someone who preferred Paul McCartney to John Lennon be at all comprehensible?

There are many who recommend escape, the simple life, as a way of managing our minds. But perhaps we deceive ourselves here, too. An acquaintance I hadn't seen for a while recently returned to town.

'What have you been up to?' I inquired.

'Oh, driving a tractor,' he said airily.

It turned out he had bought a farm, and was growing some kind of crop. He hadn't made any money, so I presumed it was a legal one. I asked what he thought of the experience.

'It's fine,' he said. 'But then I chose to do it, and I could stop when I wanted to. If I'd just ended up driving a tractor, I would have hated it like hell.'

The newspapers are full of stories about people who make millions in the finance industry, or in something to do with the internet. They suddenly see the light, and take up holistic farming, or open picture galleries. Riches and fame, it seems, don't always satisfy.

I suppose the rest of us will just have to take their word for it. I must admit to a sneaking doubt, though. Mae West, who was usually pretty straight, said that she had been poor and she had been rich. 'Rich,' she said, 'is better.'

I don't think she needed a course in meditation to work that one out.

THIS FEMINIST THING

I was on the bus, going to work, when some interesting-looking passengers got on. They were two blokes, flannelette shirts, beanies, jeans, a bit scruffy. With them, they had two children, one a baby and the other a toddler. They negotiated their entry onto the bus, always difficult with a stroller, with considerable aplomb. They had obviously done it before. They had the bag (nappies, bottles) and all the paraphernalia that inevitably attaches to going anywhere with kids. They made their way to the front group of seats and sat facing each other.

'Now,' said the older to the younger. 'What are we going to do about that fucking diff?' While the younger bloke bounced the baby on his knee and the toddler fiddled in his seat, a conversation – terse, colourful and liberally laced with expletives – ensued about a car they were repairing.

I felt greatly cheered by this experience. Men are actually quite good at childminding and even housework, if women are prepared to give them a go. But their attitude towards these tasks is completely different from ours. If you're prepared to accept men's laundry (with special lint additive), men's house cleaning (highly selective) and men's child-minding (a bit on the basic side, but on the whole they complete their shift with as many children as they started with), you are well on the way to a more satisfactory division of labour.

There may still be some men who expect their wives to work, and who do not accept any responsibility for the housework. I suspect such troglodytes to be in the minority. In most cases, the greatest obstacle to achieving more equity on the home front is not men's reluctance to get involved. It is women's reluctance to accept the standards that men think are satisfactory.

The small band of households where the woman is the breadwinner and the man does the shopping and cooking, ferries the kids about, and does the cleaning, show what can be done when there is no alternative. Where roles are reversed, there may be resentment, but there is really no argument about who should be doing what. It is in the two-income household that the battle lines are drawn. Survey after survey shows that, in two-income households, it is the woman who does most of the housework, the woman who remembers the kids' birthdays, the woman who keeps the family networks in order.

Hiring household help might appear to be at least part of the answer. But too often, the prospect of another woman plumbing the domestic dust levels proves too awful to con-template. There are practical problems, too. One man I know engaged a cleaner, but his wife spent so much time tidying the house in advance of the cleaner's arrival, they were no further ahead. As she explained, she wanted the cleaner to clean, not to tidy up. Her partner was perplexed by this. 'I don't need to pick things up before I clean,' he said. All too true. So enthusiastically did this man wield the vacuum cleaner that coins, socks, even on one occasion a pair of tights disappeared into the machine, never to be seen again.

Whatever the household arrangements, in the space of a few decades we have witnessed a social revolution in attitudes towards married women working. It was not uncommon for men of my father's generation to refuse to allow their wives to work, even when the kids were old enough not to need full-time care. Now few families can afford to be without two incomes.

But direct competition between men and women for the same jobs is constrained by a continuing occupational segregation. The workplace remains 'gendered', that is, there is very far from being a 50/50 split across all occupations. Some of these divisions have proved more amenable to change than others. Construction workers are predominantly male; hairdressers (even though these days they cut both men's and women's hair) are predominantly female. 'There are some occupations which are just blokey,' one employer said to me. He hastened to explain what he meant. (Men, at least in the public sector, have learned the importance of talking the talk.) 'If you have to wear big boots and overalls and move things around, an occupation is blokey. And women have to be blokey, too, if they want to work in those sorts of occupations.'

In an economy based largely on services and with few manufacturing jobs, women are, at least, employed. We are the new clerical proletariat. Women are the personal assistants, the office managers, the book-keepers, the receptionists. Further up the totem pole, we find women personnel managers, counsellors, and spin doctors. Many organisations have discovered that it pays to have a woman spokesperson, a softer image for dealing with the media.

But there are still not many women up the top. Even in female-dominated professions, the most senior jobs seem to go to men. The National Library of Australia, where 75 per cent of the employees are female, has only recently appointed its first woman director general. The sociologist Judy Wajcman reports that in the private sector in the US, only five per cent of managers at the top (defined as executives within three managerial levels of the CEO's job) are women. When women manage, they manage smaller groups of subordinates than men do, largely reflecting the fact that women tend to congregate in support areas like human resources and public relations, rather than in sales, finance or marketing.

It is curious, in a way, that the question of women in management is now thought to be so important. The feminist literature of the 1970s and 1980s, which equated patriarchy with capitalism, had a radical edge which has now almost completely gone. Perhaps the realisation that it is non- or pre-capitalist societies which really know how to oppress women has blunted the argument. And taste has changed, as well. Personal fulfilment, the credo of many in my genera- tion, has been replaced in our children's by a truly amazing belief in the virtues of the corporate life. The emphasis, for both men and women, is now on how to succeed in business by *really* trying.

Authorities tell us that this is no easy task. Leonie Still, in *Becoming a Top Woman Manager* advocates a no-nonsense approach. If you want to be top, she says, you must be prepared to sacrifice the lot – marriage, children, health, peace of mind. And don't get stuck in female ghettoes. Do the jobs the men do.

Of course, when the economy is organised into giant cor- porations, most men never make it to the top, either. But this may be changing. With so many internet companies springing up, rather than being famous for 15 minutes, as Andy Warhol predicted, perhaps everyone will get their 15 minutes as a CEO. But then, technology tends to be a boys' game.

What, if anything, should be done about women's under- representation at senior levels? Governments get involved in these kinds of problems at their peril, because it is so easy to do the wrong thing. For policy solutions to work as expected, there must be some congruence between the recommended action and the cause of the problem. Public servants I teach are often somewhat surprised when I point this out. They are so used to crafting political compromises they lose sight of public policy as a mechanism for change.

The most obvious, or most emotionally convenient, explanation for any given phenomenon may not be the correct one. Discrimination or prejudice against women by male managers is only one of a number of possible explanations for the lack of women senior executives. There are very few men who believe that any man is superior to any woman, although there are certainly some who believe that they, personally, are superior to every woman they encounter.

While it is conceivable that women are simply not up to the job of being a top manager, common sense suggests that it is inherently unlikely that the attributes of a successful manager are somehow under-represented among women. It is true that women are less inclined to take risks than men, but given the consequences of male entrepreneurial hubris, a degree of caution is probably no bad thing.

On the other hand, too much caution may indicate a lack of self-confidence. Many women hesitate to pursue opportunities because they are afraid they will fail. They stick to jobs which offer no real challenges because it is safer that way. It is characteristic of any group dubbed inferior – and this has been women's lot for most of recorded history – to guard jealously those activities in which it has an apparent advantage. Women may not be as ready to grasp what is on offer as men are to surrender it because, at some deep level, we lack the confidence to do so.

If we lose our supremacy in the home, but fail to advance at work, where does that leave us? For many women, the thought of men taking their place in the home is deeply threatening. Perhaps, too, this fear of displacement lies behind the stony reception men can sometimes receive when they attempt to make their way in female-dominated work-places, such as libraries or childcare centres.

Maybe doing everything is a kind of insurance policy against failure. If the glass ceiling fails to crack, we can truthfully say it was because we were unable to give the office our full attention. There were so many demands on our time.

Of course, there are other dimensions of the confidence thing. For many years, women were under the impression that it was fiendishly difficult to do top jobs. I remember reading about one woman manager who, as she laboriously scaled each successive rung in the ladder, thought that she would meet people who knew more than she did. She was surprised to find that she did not.

She was also surprised to find that at each level she was able to take the extra responsibility in her stride. The hardest part was meeting people's particular expectations of her as a boss. She was entitled to an executive parking spot, but did not use it because she did not own a car, finding it more convenient to catch the train. This just did not register. A boss was not someone who travelled by public transport. Expectations were finally met when, for other reasons, she had to buy a car.

There is little doubt that women can run things when given the chance. Women who take over when their husbands or fathers die prove that they can run the business – whether it is a newspaper group, the local mafia or a political party – just as well as the departed male, often better.

Perhaps there is a problem with qualifications, or experience? As women are reaching management levels close to the top without mishap, this seems unlikely. Is it just a matter of time? Possibly, but do not hold your breath. The proportion of women at the very top (executive directors on private sector boards) has been stuck at around 1 in 100 for nearly a decade now.

The second broad category of reasons might be called structural: women are qualified, experienced and ambitious, but are disadvantaged by unrealistic corporate demands. The higher you go, the greater the claim the organisation is assumed to have on your time and energy. In the absence of any more intelligent assessment, commitment is often judged by the number of hours on the job, which means time away from family, community and home.

To survive such an environment, managers need wives, and they need to be operating in a guilt-free environment. Men may feel deprived (or relieved) when away from their children, but they do not, as a rule, feel guilty. Socialised to think our children cannot do without us, guilt is most women's second name. I have no doubt that it holds us back. Yet we know that if we want a relationship with our children, there is no alternative to giving them our time.

The third explanation is attitudinal. Women may not think the game is worth the candle, and are deliberately saying 'no thank you' to the corporate world, where individuals are subjected to the demands of an essentially tribal culture. We may be running our own show from home, or operating in the more fluid world of small business. In the pre-factory, pre-corporate world, women often ran family businesses, or played a prominent role in them. We may still, to a far greater extent than men appear to do, want to combine career with family.

Each type of explanation suggests a different remedy. If women are ready, willing and able, and discrimination is the reason they do not get to the top, anti-discrimination legislation should be the preferred remedy. Quotas become important if anti-discrimination legislation does not do the trick. On the other hand, to the extent that structural and other factors are important, quotas will simply result in women without the necessary management skills being promoted.

Even when justified, a quota evokes the Goldilocks principle. It has to be 'just right' to work properly. Too high a level, and women are no longer being promoted on merit. Too low, and qualified women continue to miss out.

When gender becomes the basis of policy action, something rather subtle happens. When all managers were male, no man was promoted because he was a man, but rather because he was better or worse than his peers. When some managers are male and some are female, policy which acknowledges difference also creates it. It is only when managers, both male and female, define themselves in relation to their subordinates rather than to their gender that sexism disappears. Recall that when both whites and blacks were slave-traders, as was the case in West Africa in the seventeenth and eighteenth centuries, there was no racism. Both were intent on exploiting a third group – slaves – who happened to be black. It was only when there were no black exploiters, as in the slave economies of the New World, that racism was required as a legitimating ideology.

In any case, most women I know would prefer to be promoted on their own merit (a principle which could be placed at risk if quotas were set at too high a level). Even when they are not, quotas seem invidious. I recall being asked to give a paper to an academic network which happened to be all-male. I was pleased to be asked and acquitted myself reasonably well. My pleasure was, however, diminished when the senior academic involved told me, quite proudly, that he had decided to 'get a woman' to present to the network and that, undeterred by the fact that the first woman he had asked had not been available, he had kept going until he found me. It's a great life.

To be caught the other way is even worse. I recall organising a conference where, on a gender-blind selection basis, two out of the eight speakers turned out to be women. At the final session of the conference, quite unexpectedly, a woman colleague (who had said nothing to me previously) criticised the lack of gender-balance on the speakers' list. I could only say I had picked the best people for the job. But, I wondered, should I have deliberately sought out women speakers? Being mugged by the feminist conference police is a distinctly unnerving experience.

Dealing with structural problems is much more difficult than dealing with discrimination. It is necessary to change not only the rules but also the values and the resource-allocation practices of complex institutions. This requires money, time and above all, will-power. Generally the more insulated the institution is from external forces, the harder it is to change. On the whole, invigorating as opposed to enervating competition works in favour of women. If organisations were more accountable than many of them seem to be, women would not find it nearly so difficult to succeed.

The real explanation for women's under-representation seems to lie not in discrimination as such, but in the boys' club. The theory of clubs is well-established. 'You scratch my back and I'll scratch yours' is the sum of it. There are boys' citation clubs, boys' going-to-conferences clubs, and boys' let's-look-after-each-other clubs. Perhaps our competition regulators could lay off the book publishers and telephone companies, and investigate some of these arrangements, which surely must be the most anti-competitive of all.

Men are supposed to be the more competitive sex, but they are much less tough on each other than women are. Boys take each other in when times are rough. Boys give each other 'free putts'. This is the practice, described to Alistair Mant by an American chief executive, of allowing your golfing opponent a stroke or two on the green, on the understanding that he will do the same for you when you need it.

Women do not give men – or each other – free putts. One

woman manager told me that when she was promoted to head a branch in the public service, there was one employee, a man, who by manipulating the system, had been able to avoid coming to work for three years. None of his previous male bosses had been game enough to take him on. It was she who got rid of him. Women do not like loose ends.

Other problems are attributable to a coarsening of people's social imagination. In these days of the Ark syndrome, when it is ordained that people go around in couples, and at the same time the public realm is more sexualised than ever, the possibilities for other kinds of relationship are attenuated. The expectation of intimate physical relations or nothing precludes the sort of communication between men and women that is necessary for mentoring.

Those women who do manage to assume positions of power are in a no-win situation. They are scrutinised more intensely than men in the same situation, and their short-comings are more likely to be ascribed to their sex than to their personal capacities.

The trouble is that there are few valid models of female power. Whereas a powerful man is a powerful man, a woman is always both powerful and a woman. When political power is held by a woman, there must be special circumstances to justify it. Kings had to run out of male heirs before their daughters could be given a go. Joan of Arc, being of peasant stock, had to prove she was both a virgin and inspired by God. Mrs Thatcher did not have to go quite that far, but having kept her party in power for more than ten eye-popping, handbag-revving years, was disposed of more ruthlessly than any man would have been.

The fact is that we are used to male bosses. Most people, even most women, prefer a male to a female boss. Clearly we have difficulty imagining a woman boss who is neither a mother-figure or a nag. If you are consensual and 'nice', people take advantage of you. If you are as tough as old boots, you are thought unfeminine. Some women managers find it difficult to find a way of telling people what to do. One woman manager I worked for would suggest to me that 'I might like to do such and such'. It took a while to realise that these suggestions were in fact directions.

Others are terrible bullies, unnerving their male subordinates in particular, who find it difficult to reconcile normal gentlemanly modes of behaviour with telling a woman to back off. The relationship between a woman boss and a woman subordinate is particularly difficult because another woman notices, from the inside as it were, where things have not gone quite right. You can see it, the appraising stare – the inventory of make-up, hair, accessories, wrinkles, bags. Men, on the other hand, tend to subscribe to more basic forms of pattern recognition. One male friend says the only time he notices a woman's clothes is when he is thinking about taking them off.

Older women bosses find it difficult to throw off their own sexism. One I remember watched my every move, while letting a male colleague get away with murder. Younger women regularly report receiving little or no help from more senior women colleagues. Those who believe they did it on their own feel no obligation to those immediately beneath them in the power structure.

It is easy, though, to forget how much the women's movement has changed things. I remember reading a newspaper article, some thirty years ago, in the *Sydney Morning Herald*'s women's section. (That women should want, or require, a separate part of the newspaper seems odd today, although some of the writing in those sequestered pages was far more interesting than today's basic journalistic fare of financial and political speculation.)

The article purported to describe appropriate behaviour

when your car had a flat tyre. Essentially, the message was 'look pretty and some man will come and help you'. I remember thinking at the time that women were just as capable as men of changing a wheel. But if you are told that women cannot do these things, and probably should not do them, you get used to the idea.

There was discrimination everywhere. Girls couldn't play cricket. Girls couldn't deliver the mail. Girls wore shoes with pointy toes and high heels. Girls had high cheekbones and long hair, like Marianne Faithfull. Girls did not know how anything worked. Girls had to be pure, but sexy. Above all, girls had to get a bloke.

I was what used to be called a tomboy. I hated dolls (still do), didn't care about clothes (still don't), liked climbing trees, riding bikes and playing cricket (still do all three when I can get away with it). Every year, we went to my father's work Christmas party. Every year, the present for the girls was frilly, frizzy, pink and useless. The boys got something that worked, however briefly. My father tried to put me down for the boy's present, but I would have had to line up at the door that said 'boys' and in the late 1950s that was a bit radical.

Things have changed, and yet not changed. The company my father worked for, and many others like it, have disappeared, so there are not so many children's Christmas parties as there used to be. If there are, I hope the girls can get a toy car if they want one, but I imagine a little boy who wanted a doll would still have a hard time of it. Girls' choices have expanded, whereas those for boys seem to have contracted.

Thanks in part to the high-campery of the public face of male homosexuality, there is more fear and loathing of 'gays' in the boys' playground than ever before. For girls, on the other hand, a lesbian lifestyle or life-period offers a discrete way of being different, provided they can figure out what they are supposed to do with and to each other.

It is becoming increasingly apparent that boys (and men) will have to reinvent themselves if they want to compete successfully with women. The new economy is not really about technology, but communication. Boys are going to have to learn to value self-expression and listening a bit more, and watching sport a bit less, if they are going to succeed in it. This does not mean they have to model themselves on women, simply that they must acknowledge the human importance of communication.

I am not aware of any research which points to differences between the sexes which are so fundamental as to undermine such a project. Even Edward O. Wilson, the author of *Sociobiology*, is careful about the matter of gender. His most ambitious work, *Consilience*, confidently predicts a science of everything, based on a clear understanding of the way in which genes influence behaviour. But in relation to men and women he will say only that 'In aggregate, on average, with wide statistical overlap, and in many venues of social experience, they speak with a different voice.'

Even if this is true, no one can be completely sure about where the differences come from. Boys and girls play differently. The little boys run around, the little girls network. But is that innate, or just peer pressure? Left to themselves, boys are often quite interested in babies, and can talk interestingly and well. Girls like to do physical things. It is a bit like the Liberal and Labor parties – there is more variation within the parties than there is between them.

Virginia Woolf was quite certain that ultimately 'all assumptions founded on the facts observed when women were the protected sex will have disappeared'. Certainly, when I arrive home from a hard day at the office the first thing I ask my house-husband is what there is to drink and when dinner will be ready. But I must also acknowledge that, provided they don't drop dead from a heart attack in their middle years,

men have an advantage in not having to live with unpredictable, messy, depression-causing female hormones. Firstly
there is the constantly changing procession of the monthly
cycle and then the culmination of a much bigger cycle as the
whole elaborate thing laboriously shuts itself down.

It can be difficult addressing a conference of a few hundred
people while undergoing a mammoth hot flush, although I
have seen a woman weather it without apparently batting an
eyelid and emerge triumphant. Does a feminist assess the
pros and cons of hormone replacement therapy, treating it as
just another technology, or reject the whole thing as a pharmaceutical conspiracy, as Germaine Greer insists we should?
I suspect that the answers individual women will come up
with will have more to do with a pragmatic assessment of
costs and benefits than with ideology.

Maybe that is feminism's greatest achievement – to expose
as convention what was previously thought to be the natural
state of affairs, and to give women more choices as a result.
Perhaps, too, women now have more confidence to search
for better answers to the problems which remain and to
share their experiences in dealing with them. Women confronting the terror of breast cancer are no longer so alone as
they once were. Post-natal depression is talked about more
openly. When most women's husbands die before them,
women have become, sadly, the experts in grief and grieving.

Women have always been the unofficial counsellors and
carers – now they are likely to be the professionals in the
field. It is only where men claim some form of charismatic
authority that women find themselves excluded. Witness
the irony of the male priest presiding over a dwindling,
predominantly female congregation.

Meanwhile, young girls are more likely to wear Doc
Martens than stilettos, a development no doubt applauded by
podiatrists and the owners of parquet floors. But do young

girls assume that they will have to provide for a family? They had better believe it. Women are more and more likely to find themselves in the situation of supporting men.

An acquaintance of mine had just been through a very messy divorce which, so she told me, had cost her a packet. (With more women working, husbands too have the opportunity of cleaning up in the Family Court.) Anyway, as a result of this, she had gone into business for herself, with the avowed intention of making lots of money. 'I never used to think money was important,' she said. 'I always went where my heart was. But at some point, that attitude catches up with you, doesn't it? You find you want different things, and you can't have them.' I guess this is what equality means.

The French courtesan Ninon de Lenclos, although well advanced in years herself, is said to have taken much younger lovers. As women assume more economic power, I am waiting for this trend to emerge, but it will take time. When *New Idea* bursts with photos of male bimbos hanging on the arms of wealthy, powerful and older women, we'll know we've made it.

SPEAKING OUT

We all know the scene. The hero is up on the stage, about to give an important speech. He has something prepared, something boring, safe and appropriate. He starts to intone the words, but something is not quite right. He thrusts the prepared speech aside or, more dramatically, tears it in half. He decides to speak from the heart instead.

The audience, resigned to hearing the expected words, starts to take an interest. Here is something unusual, something risky. Perhaps some evil is exposed, some conspiracy denounced. Perhaps it is just that the mask of convention is removed, however briefly, and a person rather than a mouthpiece stands revealed. Someone is speaking out.

It is a fantasy, of course, but a common one. At a personal level, in our relations with others, we censor what we say. Feelings might be hurt; we fear retaliation; there is nothing to be gained and much to lose.

'Never burn your bridges' is everyone's favourite piece of advice. But it all depends who is on the other side when you try to go back. People don't stay long in their jobs these days, so a fiery exit does not necessarily stay long in the corporate memory. Or there may have been a palace revolution since your departure, and those who were in are now out, and vice versa.

In any case, people are so busy, some at least forget who has offended them and who hasn't, so provided you pick your time and place, a little speaking out may do you the world of good without harming your prospects. As ever, family members are more tricky. The anthropologists (or is it the sociologists?) tell us that it all depends upon that handy carry-all, family culture. Some families enjoy a good set-to, no holds barred, helps to clear the air. Others Hold Grudges. But the modern world has taken the sting out of the old-fashioned family feud. They used to be sombre, intergenerational sagas, continued long after the primary cause had been forgotten. Now, in the era of the five-second sound-bite, they take more concentration than most people can summon. In any case, as with so many things people used to do for themselves, the professionals have taken over. If we want to see people speaking out, we can always see them doing it on TV, where they say the sorts of things we might have said to each other if we weren't so busy watching TV.

Nevertheless, there are times when we feel we really must, out of respect for ourselves, say something. How we love to rehearse our lines! A friend told me how, in the course of an extremely traumatic house extension, her builder took the roof off part of the house and then left for the day. Overnight, the skies opened, the room was inundated, the carpet a soggy mess. The builder appeared the next day, cheery as ever. 'That's a beauty isn't it,' he said, surveying the soaked floor covering. 'Now,' thought my friend, 'I'll tell him exactly what I think of him.' But somehow her nerve failed her, and her speech of an outraged householder was never delivered. The builder took up the carpet and disappeared with it. It was returned a few days later, dry, but still a bit bedraggled. 'There, looks as good as new,' he announced. To her amazement, she found herself agreeing that it 'wasn't too bad'.

Another friend took his car to have a routine service done at the local service station. When he returned to pick it up, his car did not look the same as when he left it. The mechanic had a strange tale to relate. He had, he said, put the car on the hoist but had been distracted by something, and forgotten to close the door first. As the car sped towards the ceiling, there was a terrific bang. 'Jesus,' the mechanic said. 'At first I thought it was the terrists.' It turned out that the car window had shattered as it collided with the side of the shed and the impact had twisted the door as well.

'Not to worry,' said the mechanic, the window would be replaced and no, he would not charge for the oil change either.

'What did you say?' I asked my friend.

'What could I say?' he replied. 'I just muttered something about these things happening. At least he told me the truth, which is more than most of them do.'

Even in the classless society of Oz, speaking out is a bit of a luxury. In his expose of life at St Andrew's College at the University of Sydney between 1991 and 1995, Peter Cameron had some revealing things to say about Australians. Cameron was forced to resign as Principal of the College because (among other things) he advocated the admission of women students.

The traditionalist opposition to him, he recalled, revolved around a few 'key Councillors' (members of the College's governing body), who made sure they had the numbers when and where it counted. Their behaviour was as predictable as their methods were underhand.

What really disappointed him, though, was the timidity of his supporters. 'They would often fail at the last minute to come to meetings which they knew would be crucial, and at the meetings they did attend they would sit silent and shame-faced,' he wrote. 'And afterwards over a drink they would say privately to me, with enormous passion and indignation, everything they should have said at the meeting.'

Cameron speculated that while Australians are not lacking in physical courage, we may be a little lacking in moral fibre. I am not sure whether this is true or not, and it is a statement which would be impossible to test scientifically.

But at some level, Cameron's comments ring true. While we like to think of ourselves as plain-speaking people, ever prepared to call a spade a spade, I am not sure that many of us would be prepared to do this if the prevailing view was that a spade was something else.

There may be structural explanations for some of this. Australia is not a populous country, and each of the state capitals offers a small, surprisingly self-contained, power centre. It is not easy to stand up to powerful people if the likely result of doing so is some curtailment of one's own prospects. Dissent is easier in societies where there are numerous alternative avenues of employment.

After all, it took a fish and chip shop lady with a quavering voice to change politics in Australia. After years of listening to public utterances which all sounded pretty much the same, the populace was amazed to hear someone actually saying something different. Like most self-employed people, Pauline Hanson's politics were of the right-wing rather than the left-wing variety. Had she announced the dictatorship of the proletariat on that day in Canberra, no one would have batted an eyelid (although possibly the voters of Ipswich who had elected her to parliament would have been a little taken aback). But to say Aborigines should receive no special favours, that multiculturalism was offensive to the Anglo majority, and that our immigration intake included too many Asians was far more shocking.

Pauline was able to speak out because she did not want a job with the government, did not hanker for a seat on a board, did not particularly care whether she was liked or not, and had never been to university. There have been many first speeches in the House before and since. It is a measure of the paltry party-bound thing parliament has become that none has had anything like the impact of Pauline's effort.

There can be no doubt that many Australians agreed with Pauline's views, including some who would never admit to it publicly. There were many others who did not agree with her views, but thought it important that they should be discussed. There never was much discussion, because we haven't yet found a way of talking about cultural difference in a way which acknowledges the fact that people of one culture generally feel more at home with others who share their basic values and beliefs.

Our age has brought a lot out into the open. We can say just about anything we like about sex and superannuation. Childbirth is on open show. Some women I know have more people in the delivery room than Louis XIV at one of his levees. But we can no more talk about immigration than the agonies of choosing bathroom tiles.

If Hegel was right, that progress is achieved through the contest of ideas, we are in deep trouble. We will never know what advantages a multicultural society might have until we have learned to talk freely about a monocultural one. And we will never understand either while we continue to think of race and culture as the same thing.

Universities, or more accurately, the people who work in them, should be helping to forge the intellectual and verbal tools which will enable us to grasp some of these things and think about them more clearly. But unfortunately, universities are the last places one would look for any kind of originality, creativity or even (with a few honourable exceptions) just plain speaking in these matters.

If you work in a university, there is an invisible wall around you. I sense it, I think everyone does. There are certain things you cannot say, cannot even think. It is a world where people wear labels, or have them applied to them. The labels all come from other times, other places. But you cannot get rid of them.

Politically correct people have always made me feel uncomfortable. For years, I thought this was because they possessed moral insights I did not have. But now I am not so sure. We need people to remind us of where we have strayed, where we might do better. But problems occur when a certain kind of speaking out becomes institutionalised. When the state starts lecturing people, it is time to find a new state.

It is a curious thing that the average Australian would probably give the shirt off his back to help an individual refugee down on his luck, while feeling personally and collectively affronted by the thought of boatloads of illegals bearing down on Christmas Island. At the same time, I can think of few of the politically correct who I would describe as compassionate at the individual, face-to-face level. They are much more comfortable with the idea of humanity in the abstract.

For years at the Australian National University, I was made fun of because I dared to suggest that, on the whole, Anglo-celtic Australian culture was not something of which one ought to be ashamed. I was forced to express myself more forcefully than I otherwise would have done because I could not bear to hear something I loved being so traduced.

In this sort of climate, one finds oneself speaking out without really meaning to. I belong to the great kingdom of the contrarians. Whatever you say, I will find something to say against it. If you say the unemployed are terrible bludgers, I will find reasons why that is a bit harsh. If you say they are saintly people, I will argue against that, too. I can't help it.

Do you know that feeling when you read something, and

you understand exactly what the other person means? I had that experience recently when I was reading Montaigne. In one of his essays, he describes how he liked to talk, playfully, in an exploratory fashion, without having to worry too much about saying the wrong thing. But we should always choose the right people with whom to have these kinds of conversations.

I have had terrible arguments with people I regard as friends. We should always agree with our friends, because to disagree risks the friendship – for what? What does it matter what your opinions are, or mine? They will not change any-thing. And if they could, we would no doubt try to be much better-informed.

One of the key debates we never seem to have is how tough or otherwise we should be in public policy matters. Open-ended compassion is dangerous stuff for governments, as it is to varying degrees for individuals, too. My father used to speak of the principle of thirds: one-third of any group of people will work hard in a job, do a bit more than a fair day's work for a fair day's pay. Another third will do exactly what you have paid them to do – no more and no less. And the final third will, for various reasons, find all sorts of ways to rip you off. The difficult bit is working out who is who.

As a teacher I have found, the hard way, that feeling sorry for people and making allowances for them does not do them, or me, much good. I remember one year I was marking essays until Christmas because I had given so many exten-sions. Good policy is one's only defence. Now I spell out, quite clearly, the circumstances under which I will grant an extension. This requires a fair bit of knowledge and experi-ence. Then comes the hard part. You have to actually stick to it. Most people will play by the rules, if the rules are fair and are properly enforced. Some people are just too disorganised to conform. They are in some ways the most difficult cases, because they usually cop the penalty without too much complaint. Then there are those who don't really believe you meant what you said. The essay comes in late with a carefully penned plea for lenience, or a scrawled doctor's certificate covering just one day (a sure sign the doctor smelt a rat), or several days, but after the essay was due.

You get through all this, and then a student you have barely seen during the unit turns up with a story of family trauma which has prevented him or her from doing any work (although not from doing their regular job). They are so far outside the rules, my carefully defined line in the sand looks quite ludicrous.

There are tensions between compassion, consistency and even effectiveness that bedevil any field of decision-making that involves people. When is an asylum seeker a refugee, and when is he an economic migrant? When is a worker an employee, when a genuine contractor? When is an unemployed person a bludger whose benefits should be withdrawn, and when an unfortunate victim of circumstance? Consistent decision-making requires categories, cut-off dates, criteria, but people are more complex than such frameworks can accommodate, and too zealous an application of the rules can easily lead to injustice.

Speaking out may help politicians and administrators to think more clearly about some of these issues, but not if speaking out means ignoring the real dilemmas that are involved. Australians don't like political exhibitionism, to use Bob Carr's term, and they are suspicious of those who take the moral high ground at no cost to themselves. On the other hand, too much understanding can be as bad as too little. We don't take back the cold cup of coffee or the bad meal. We think, 'They are probably doing their best. What's the point of speaking up?' The bad cup of coffee was probably made by someone who did not know how to make a good one, anyway.

It takes courage to be critical. I have only ever heard one senior manager say that he deliberately seeks out the dissenters when he takes over a new organisation. 'They're usually the ones who care,' he told me. He was one of the confident ones, willing to hear about what his predecessors had done or left undone. I wondered, though, whether he would remain interested once the dissenters were critical of him.

The giving of advice is fraught with risk. On a number of occasions, thinking I was being helpful, I offered to comment on colleagues' work for them. I praised, but was also critical. This was not welcomed. One advisee even refused to speak to me – I ended up apologising to her for being too outspoken. On another occasion, one of the contributors to a collection of papers I was editing threatened to report me to the union for refusing to publish his chapter as he had submitted it. He later told me, on re-reading this effort, that he found it embarrassingly bad.

Not many people are interested in getting it right, because to be both fair and accurate takes time, intelligence and a willingness to follow a line of inquiry, wherever it may lead. John Donne in his 'Satyre: on religion' pictured truth with his customary panache, an image I have never forgotten:

> On a huge hill
> Cragged and steep, Truth stands, and hee that will
> Reach her, about must, and about must go;
> And what the hills suddenness resists, winne so.

The American academic Aaron Wildavsky, who thought brilliantly and wrote better, once described policy advising as 'speaking truth to power'. In British and Australian parlance this approximates to the phrase 'frank and fearless advice'. Public servants are supposed to tell ministers not what they want to hear, but what they need to know. I would have thought that having an honest, experienced and well-informed person whom you could call upon, at any time of the night or day, to give you dispassionate advice on whatever problem was confronting you, was the most wonderful privilege. But public servants of this stamp are less popular with most politicians than an Arab in a flying school.

Advisers you can trust must be worth their weight in gold. Trust comes in two forms. There are advisers you know will be loyal to you and will do their best for you because they know that their career sinks or swims with yours. Then there are advisers who will serve you professionally and do their best for you because that is their job.

When just about everyone has an interest to protect, where is independence to come from? Consultants are hoping for the next job. Bureaucrats are hoping to keep their current one. It is not just those employed on contract who are affected. Semi-voluntary redundancies are a great way to keep people in line.

The people who know most about what is going on, usually have the most incentive to conceal it. Australia's virtually non-existent tradition of investigative journalism (except when it comes to restaurant reviews) means that they can be fairly sure no one will find out – unless someone blows the whistle.

Whistleblowers have a terrible time, because although a climate of corruption may reek to high heaven, the legal system works on cases, places and faces. Ted Steele of Wollongong University, who was sacked for misconduct when he signed a statutory declaration asserting that two fee-paying honours students had been passed when in his judgment they should have failed, simply drew attention to what every academic knows to be the case – standards at Australian universities have been falling steadily over the past 20 years, and those applied to international fee-paying students (both on-shore and offshore) are in many cases lower still. Academics bend over backwards to pass these students, not because they have been specifically directed to do so (although this has certainly happened) but because they know that, in an offshore teaching situation for example, if they fail half the class, questions will be asked, and they may well have their competence as teachers impugned. Ted Steele eventually got his job back, when a court found that the University had wrongly dismissed him. Yet who among us has not felt that the line of least resistance was the best way out of a difficult situation?

As is usual in these matters, when frank and fearless are most needed, they are least likely to appear. (I imagine frank and fearless to be two rather portly gentlemen of identical demeanour, a bit like the Mr Cherubles in *Nicholas Nickleby*. They are up front when they do appear, but too often they get written out of the script.) A corrupt government will ensure that it never hears what it needs to know because in becoming corrupt, or continuing to be corrupt, it will have ensured that no one likely to tell it how it is, survives.

Sometimes it is not speaking out which is required, but simply a preparedness to say 'are you sure?' I am a great advocate of people asking questions. Many of us are afraid to do it because, unless the question is rhetorical or simply asked for the purpose of showing off, the questioner is asking about something which he or she does not know or does not understand.

This is difficult to do, because it actually takes a fair bit of understanding to begin to give an outline to what you don't know, and even more to make a credible link with the person who has been giving the presentation. This is where that mysterious quality called intelligence comes in. An intelligent presenter will not pull apart or make fun of the malformed question, but will do the questioner the courtesy of trying to understand where he or she is coming from. What particular area of puzzlement is driving the query?

Only the exceptionally self-confident are not afraid of being thought foolish, which is one of the main reasons that con-artists and certain businesspeople and even some academics are able to get away with so much. No one is game to say 'what are you talking about?' or 'what does that figure there mean?', and when the answer fails to satisfy, to say so, and to make them go through it again.

Most of the time, we stumble through a fog of ambiguity, and much of what we say is not clear or is clear only to ourselves, speaking from that immaculate dug-out we call our minds. So practise, in front of the mirror if need be. 'Would you mind going through that again?'

How do we challenge power and survive? The first answer is that it cannot be done alone, and the second is not to go off half-cocked. The third is to remember you don't have to make a full-frontal assault. Think of the technique of the court jester, the fool, who manages to take the mickey out of his employer without having his head separated from his shoulders, unless he goes too far.

At some level, as a Tibetan lama with a grasp of the local idiom said to me, if you stick your neck out, you must be prepared to suffer the consequences. Check your motivation first, was his advice, because speaking out for the wrong reason can put you, rather than your adversary, in the hot-seat.

But being overly sure can lead to paralysis, and no one ever fully understands their own motivation. Just for once, for the sake of plain dealing amidst all the hypocrisy; for the sake of the hopes you may once have had or never dared to have; if for no other reason than you have never done it before – take a deep breath, get hold of your lines, and let 'em have it.

THE AMERICANS, MATE

In 1966, during the Vietnam War, the photographer David Moore took a famous picture of Australian Prime Minister Harold Holt and the American President Lyndon Baines Johnson standing together on an official dais at Canberra Airport. Johnson is speaking, leaning on a lectern, a big confident craggy man, a Texan in the White House. And then behind him, quietly waiting his turn, is Harold Holt, a small dapper man looking down at his impeccably polished shoes.

It would be tempting to see Holt as the menial in the relationship, but such an impression would be misleading. Harold is actually quite pleased with himself, and not only because he has attracted a serving American President to these shores. We now know that the Australian government feared the southward push of Communism so much that it not only supported the American presence in Vietnam, it egged the Americans on as much as it could.

Whether the war made sense for either country was beside the point. As far as most people were concerned, if the Americans were there, we had to be there too. Opposition at that time carried a heavy political price. In 1966 there was an election at which the Australian Labor Party, led by Arthur Caldwell, took a principled stand against the war, and the conscription that fed it. Australia, said Caldwell, had no business being in Vietnam. He was right, of course, but in politics there are no prizes for being ahead of public opinion.

The election was lost in a landslide, and Caldwell, one of the last of the old-style Labor politicians of the Chifley era, stepped down as leader, to be replaced by Gough Whitlam, a man whose views on the war were well to the right of Caldwell's, but who represented, more than any other, the aspirations of middle class Australia. As Groucho Marx might have said, if you can fake those, you've got it made.

Thirty-seven years on, and in the Australian autumn of 2003, John Howard is the Liberal leader. The Americans have, depending upon your point of view, either invaded, or liberated Iraq. In contrast to Vietnam, where they drifted into the conflict over a number of years before becoming hopelessly bogged down, in Iraq the Americans became bogged down almost immediately, having announced their intention to unseat its leader, the unsavoury Saddam Hussein, well in advance. Although Saddam fled the scene, one suspects the longer-term result of the Americans' action will be to install a far more hard-line Islamic regime than Saddam's, a pretty standard all-purpose tyranny, without any conspicuous religious legitimation.

Australian troops were there from the outset, although such is the compulsive secrecy of the Australian military, hardly anyone was aware of the fact. This may prove handy in the days to come but was frustrating at the time. When the war was at its hottest, our boys might as well have been on the moon for all the news that Australian taxpayers received of them.

But let us return to John Howard. His economics and, I suspect, much of his politics, would be quite alien to Harold Holt, who preferred scuba diving to cricket, had married a divorcee and, in any case, came from Melbourne. John Howard might in fact have felt more at home in the 1950s than Harold Holt did, but he is nevertheless too shrewd a politician to say anything crassly subservient to, or about, George Bush. In any case, it is harder to find suitable words to rhyme with 'Bush'.

For a man like Howard, there was little choice about following the Americans into the war. He is a conservative, with a shrewd political touch, and he sees a natural congruence of worldview between us and the Americans. (The fact that Tony Blair threw in his lot with George added an irresistible dash of English-speaking group-think to the brew.)

Howard's government had, without fanfare, already prepared the ground. In its 1997 White Paper, *In the National Interest*, the government underlined the importance of Australia's economic and security engagement with the United States. Australia's security was underwritten by the alliance with the United States which also conferred important economic benefits, largely in the form of access to technology.

But I would suggest that even for a less conservative Prime Minister than John Howard, the choice not to have joined the Americans in Iraq would have been a difficult one. Thirty-seven years on from Harold Holt's 'All the way with LBJ', in an Australia remade by global capitalism and utterly different in sensibility, what matters is, still, the American alliance.

This is not to say that it matters all the time. The American alliance, as the international relations scholar T.B. Millar pointed out, is a sort of insurance policy, fairly cheap in terms of premiums (although matters got a little out of hand in Vietnam), but payments are required only intermittently, depending upon what the Americans are up to.

Most of the time, Australia goes its own way, or ways. The intersecting and overlapping fields of international relations, foreign, defence, trade and immigration policy are characteristically the province of insiders – those in government, and those with the ear of government. Public opinion may guide tactics, but rarely strategy, unless something goes wrong.

But when the American alliance is invoked, like a giant lodestone, it draws the compass needle of the Australian ship of state far from its usual course. If Australia had no real business to be in Vietnam, it is harder to discern any rationale, other than the alliance, for being in Iraq. (The Coalition might have reasoned that such a move would be unlikely to harm Australia's chances in its continuing efforts to secure a bilateral free trade deal with the Americans, but a formal quid pro quo seems most unlikely).

Since the Vietnam War, as Donald Rumsfeld, the American Secretary of Defence might say, some stuff has happened. The first major piece of stuff was that the Soviet Union, a colossus that once bestrode the top half of the world and much of eastern and central Europe besides, collapsed, and was replaced by a strange country ruled, as much of the west is, by media barons and their political allies. This country is known internationally as Russia.

It has become the conventional wisdom of many Americans, and a source of at least some of their contemporary hubris, that it is they who caused the Soviet Union to turn into Russia. The mighty edifice, they believe, was brought down by relentless pressure from a crusading president in the form of Ronald Reagan, who was not afraid to put other people's money where his mouth was. The reality was a lot more complex.

If you travelled across the Soviet Union in the latter part of the Brezhnev era, three things were immediately apparent. The first was that this was not an advanced industrial society. The second was that hardly anyone believed in the official ideology. The third was that most of the male population appeared to be permanently drunk. Many countries have at least one of these characteristics, and some have two and manage to survive. But three are bound to prove fatal.

This was a country where mechanisation had barely reached many farms; where the streets were swept by solid looking old ladies dressed in black; a country where the shops were empty of both goods and people, and where whole cities were sealed off, their inhabitants bent on the construction of what would now be called weapons of mass destruction.

The only bright spot seemed to be the performing arts, which were incomparable. All forms of knowledge and opinion were strictly controlled, and English language books were doled out one at a time in foreign language bookshops to readers who had to identify themselves before they could purchase them. Occasionally, motorcades of dark cars with dark glass concealing the occupants would sweep down streets specially cleared of traffic for the purpose. People's faces were impassive, but in private and in the freely circulating samizdat or underground literature they made it quite plain what they thought of their rulers.

Eventually the sclerotic leaders of the late 1970s were replaced by those, like Gorbachev, who understood that matters could not go on as they had been. But as fast as Gorbachev attempted to replace the rotten timbers of the old regime with something more serviceable, the house fell down around him. Reagan's spending on defence undoubtedly increased the pressure on the old order, but it would surely have collapsed anyway.

No matter – the Americans had recovered the self-confident belief, the conviction, that their destiny was not to accommodate to the Soviets, but to prove their superiority to them. Australia does not produce conviction politicians. It is not our style. But Mrs Thatcher showed everyone what was possible when you just knew you were right.

Ronald Reagan went one better, by demonstrating that conviction worked better than policy every time. The difficulty was in working out whose convictions they in fact were. Like George W. Bush, Reagan seemed to be acting for others. The difference was that Reagan did not need to connect mentally with his mentors in order to say his lines beautifully. George Bush does know what his lines mean, but struggles to articulate them convincingly.

The second piece of stuff that happened was September 11 2001. Actually, there were two dates. The first was September 11, when for the first time in its history as an independent nation, foreigners took their fight with the United States onto its own soil.

Then there was the eleventh of September 2001, a rainy day in early spring in south-eastern Australia, in fact the last decent rain before the terrible drought of 2002 set in. I have vivid memories of that day, because the stormwater pipes were overfull, causing the cellar under the house to flood. After an anxious night I rushed down to the hire shop the following morning to hire a pump, and was unable to attract the attention of either of the two salespersons, who were glued to their TV sets watching a scene of incomprehensible destruction. The eleventh of September turned into September 11, and was never the same again. The American nightmare somehow became our nightmare, too.

September 11 made the Americans realise, not that they were not universally loved, for no nation that had inflicted Bruce Willis movies on the world could expect that, but that there were people in the world who actively loathed them and all they stood for, and felt that hatred sufficiently strongly to want to kill them. The Soviets, when they were around, had at least played the game. Now the Americans learned there were worse things than communism. (And the Europeans, contemplating the brutal ethnic wars of Bosnia and Kosovo, learned there were some things worse even than terrorism.)

History tells us that where American interests are involved, and American power is unconstrained, few niceties are observed. It is a tradition which goes back to the earliest period of independence. On his first visit to the Falkland Islands, in 1833, Charles Darwin found the residents of Port Louis, the rudimentary capital run at that time by the Argentinians, still reeling from the depredations of the USS *Lexington* which, in 1831, had destroyed both property and buildings and taken prisoner a number of the residents, because they had interfered with the activities of some American sealers.

The revenge of the Americans was similarly swift and terrible in 2001, descending first on the Taliban, who had harboured Osama bin Laden, and then on Saddam, who almost certainly had not. The Americans were acting towards the rest of the world as they had long done in Central and South America – strike hard, and do not ask questions at any time.

Like many people throughout the world, Australians grieved with the Americans when their shiny towers, and the thousands of people working within them, were destroyed. But for a people tied by a continuing alliance with the Americans, some questions were working their way to the surface. They had been the good guys when it mattered, and it was hard to see what hope there was for the world if they were no longer the good guys. But were the Americans, many of us wondered uneasily, still unequivocally the good guys? On what basis were they permitted to have weapons of mass destruction, but everyone else was allowed only weapons of ordinary destruction?

We see America as a culture, but in fact it is its political system that should be causing Australians concern. The country we are allied with in 2003 is not the same as the United States of the middle 1960s. What economist John Kenneth Galbraith called the 'countervailing power' of organised labour is much weakened, and the financial requirements of winning office, in a media-dominated age, are much greater than in the past. Despite efforts to limit campaign expenditures, the financial resources of business and of powerful religious and other interests buy influence in the Congress and in the Presidency to an unprecedented degree. Very few politicians, of whatever political persuasion, escape the thrall of corporate donors. In the case of the Bush administration, the links between big business and the White House are so close as to be indivisible.

Many Americans are in despair about the power of special interest groups in their democracy. As legal academic Ronald Dworkin wrote in the *New York Review of Books* in 1996, 'the influence of wealth unequally distributed is greater, and its consequences more profound, than at any time in the past'. The problem has, if anything, worsened since then. Being allied with the Americans is one thing. Being allied with American business is another.

In 2003, the ultra-conservative Republican Right, with its close business connections, is in the ascendant. It may not stay that way for long, but for its numbers, it exerts a much stronger influence on policy than would be the case for an equivalent movement in Australia.

Australia adheres, very rightly in my view, to the Rousseau-esque proposition that we should be forced to be free. We have compulsory voting. In the United States, it is actually quite difficult to vote. You have to register as a voter of a particular party, the polls are held on a weekday, and of course, if you don't vote, no one cares.

What this means is that the people who have most to gain from wise government do not cast their votes, and the outcome is skewed in favour of those who have most to gain from the horse-trough of government, who are generally the rich. How else to explain the endless succession of tax cuts that have widened inequality and impoverished public services since the time of Ronald Reagan?

Iraq will fade into the welter of local sympathies and priorities that will determine its future. America, too, will no doubt enter a more quiescent period. But what does the underlying higher level of risk mean for Australian foreign policy? Unlike the Americans, our independence did not have to be fought for. But it does have to be thought for.

When the Americans are not involved, and without the steady pressure of a well-developed business interest, the Australian ship of state heels to the prevailing winds. As the veteran academic commentator Coral Bell noted in the early 1990s, in no other field of policy are the priorities and per-sonality of the prime minister as important as in foreign policy. After Gough Whitlam brought the boys back from Vietnam, Malcolm Fraser ushered into Australia over 100,000 Vietnamese refugees, fleeing from a regime Australia had fought, unsuccessfully, against. Fraser did little to change trade policy, an oversight for which he has since been mercilessly hammered by the econocrats. Labor under Hawke, the ulti-mate pragmatist, pursued a reformist agenda in the economy and the public service and, anxious to spread its multilateral message as far as possible, pursued a program of relentless activism in trade matters.

This was the era of APEC, Asia-Pacific Economic Cooperation, when Australia 'punched above its weight' in international affairs. APEC was a noble ideal but destined never to be quite as important to the other participants as it was to Australia. It eventually faded, leaving only a memory of heads of state in unflattering shirts.

Australia's own gonzo foreign affairs minister, Gareth

Evans, co-authored, while still in office, a book on Australia's foreign relations which soon became the definitive account of the period. Evans crafted the busyness of his ministry into a special tapestry – Cambodia saved, special relationship with Ali Alatas, the Indonesian Foreign Minister, finessed. Australia was now 'enmeshed' with Asia. But even Gareth failed to appreciate the full implications of the critical event, the demise of the Soviet Union in the later 1980s and early 1990s.

John Howard's great political strength was to divine just how sick Australians were of the self-congratulatory hype of this period. They hated Keating, they had had a gutful of multiculturalism, and many thought it was high time the Aborigines stopped blaming white Australia for all their problems.

There were opportunities in foreign policy as well. What better way to make the break complete than by taking the lead on East Timor once Suharto was out of the way? And what better way to signal that traditional ties were in the ascendant than by resuscitating the American alliance? Which is where we came in.

In retrospect, forty years of Australian policy-making constitutes an odd melange of sentiment, doctrine and self-interest. From our neighbours' perspective, the oscillations must be puzzling. Self-interest they can understand; changing conceptions of self-interest they can understand. But the quixotic compulsion must be hard to come to terms with. After years of dalliance with the Indonesians, Australia was on the side of the angels in East Timor, sent peace-keeping troops to Bougainville and the Solomons, but seems to have forgotten the existence of Papua New Guinea, our very own ex-colonial state, now on the verge of complete disintegration.

Meanwhile, what were the defence planners to do? Simply put, if you are going to have an independent foreign policy, you need to be able to defend yourself. That means, in turn, having a defence force that is constituted and trained with that end in mind. Bipartisan support and a sense of steady purpose is required, because in international affairs, as we have seen, there is much to distract the Australian leader keen to make his mark in history or at least to make his presence felt in foreign capitals.

Unfortunately, there was no such sense of steady purpose, and Defence planners have had a difficult time of it in the years since Vietnam. The strategic blueprint known as the Dibb report concentrated on credible threats, and concluded that there were none. But the Dibb report was published in 1986, before the end of the bipolar world, when it was possible to construct a policy without reference to the Americans.

Then, in the early 1990s, Australia was involved in a succession of United Nations-led peace-keeping forces, in Cambodia, Somalia and Rwanda. Peace-keeping forces are very different from conventional military forces, being more lightly armed and, depending upon the role they have been assigned, containing a higher proportion of specialist personnel such as doctors and communications experts. For a country keen on getting involved but not keen on paying for the necessary flexibility, meeting these demands must have imposed heavy stresses on those required to do the actual work.

To have a foreign policy means, presumably, to have a considered stance towards other countries, based on a model of the world which gives a credible place to one's own. What is that model?

Unfortunately, owing to our own period of McCarthyism, the era of political correctness, the only real thinking has come from the economists. The mantra of competitive markets may have given us the world's greatest economy, but in a world of more than 180 nation states, it has given us few political concepts to work with. The international relations scholars do a lot of creative finger-painting, but are reluctant to develop a point of view that is practically useful. Their favourite debate – the extent to which the behaviour of nation states is explained by self-interest – is of little help to those wanting creative ideas for conceptualising Australia's place in the world.

The dreadful pall of political correctness may have lifted, but the ambit of public debate remains pathetically limited, largely because so few Australians know anything about what happens inside the black box of government. Our parliaments are nobbled by party-political control, our media by savage defamation laws and concentrated ownership, and our courts by ramifying thickets of executive adjudication. The ultimate pragmatists, perhaps we are sensible to keep so much hidden away: to allow politicians to treat parliament as a joke; to put up with newspapers and TV that lack the resources or the appetite for investigation; to entrust our rights to commissions, tribunals and boards. But the price seems to be that we rely on other people's wars to help us work out who we are.

Should we retain the American alliance? The Canadians do not need it, and the New Zealanders lost it because of their anti-nuclear convictions. Indeed, since being kicked out of ANZUS, they have gone from strength to strength. They won the America's Cup (twice!), and only lost it at the beginning of 2003 when they let the other team have a Kiwi skipper as well. In the meantime, they made *The Lord of the Rings*, invented the Kiwi fruit, and voted in the first woman Australasian prime minister. Recently, a New Zealand military man told me that their Minister for Disarmament outranks the Minister for Defence in the Cabinet.

It would be bracing to go in the same direction. But Australian geography is unique. New Zealand is unlikely to be invaded – it is difficult enough to find coming from the north as it is. Australia, too, is unlikely to be invaded, but our part of the world is much more unstable.

Perhaps the answer to our questions about the Americans lies less in geopolitical considerations, and more in cultural ones. Perhaps we find it difficult to be as clear-minded in our dealings with them as we need to be, because we are less like them than we suppose.

Like them, we are multicultural; we have a burgeoning meritocracy and are unashamedly materialistic. Australian English is disappearing under the weight of American imports. (The acid test, I think, will be when we start referring to the boot of a car as the 'trunk'.) But the defining forces of history and geography make for more fundamental differences.

We inhabit a big, empty, largely barren continent, and we have always felt that what we have is tenuous, even, perhaps, not entirely legitimate. We did not start auspiciously: Australia was settled by felons, second sons and assisted migrants. But don't think of coming here uninvited, and don't try to make us feel guilty about anything, okay?

Americans are congenitally patriotic, even or perhaps especially, the poorest and most disadvantaged among them. Australians are gradually learning the words of the national anthem and can sing it in public, although still rather shyly.

We take sport so seriously we can even bear to lose some-times. We don't invent much technology, but we do fireworks and public extravaganzas like the Olympics better than just about anyone else. We have fought to defend our way of life in the past, and would do so again, but although we know, almost palpably, what it is to be Australian, we are not good at putting it into words.

We think God has probably heard of us, but we don't hold with bothering her, if we can help it. We are pagans, which means we go in for tribal bonding rather than charity. We help our mates, and we help the poor (through the state). But we don't believe that they have any right to our attention, or our money.

We might think the neighbours are bastards, but the word 'evil' does not come readily to our lips. The smiling, smooth-faced bomb-maker of Bali aroused our anger and contempt, but we are not a people given to metaphysical explanations. It is hard work to get Australians to love anyone, but at the same time it is hard to get us to hate them, either.

We are not a militaristic people, but we do go on rather a lot about the wars we have been involved in, more than any other country I can think of. From being almost an embarrassment in my youth, Anzac Day has become chic, despite or maybe even because of the fact that the men who formed the basis of the legend, the Diggers of the First and Second World Wars, have almost all gone from us.

And here, perhaps, there is a very important contrast. An individualistic, competitive and impatient culture, such as the American, does not have much time for war. In fact, they want to get ouda there as quickly as they can. Think of the manic nihilism of *Catch 22*, or the crazy helicopters and the brooding Brando character of *Apocalypse Now*. War brings out the Australian sense of the tragic – think of the pointlessness of the final charge in Peter Weir's film of *Gallipoli*, as the young men go heroically, knowingly, to their deaths.

Real war, of course, is different. The First World War was too dreadful, even for stories. But of those old soldiers I knew who survived the Second, it was an account written by Douglas McLaggan of surviving the horrors of the Burma Railway that sticks in my mind. The Australians survived, he said, when others perished, by working together, and by helping each other. I hope we can keep those collectivist traditions alive, whatever lies ahead of us.

Perhaps Australian irony and American triumphalism, Australian pessimism and American optimism, Australian mateship and American individualism can in some way form a partnership for peace, rather than a tag team for war. Let's hope so.

Avagoodweegend.

Wakefield Press is an independent publishing and
distribution company based in Adelaide, South Australia.
We love good stories and publish beautiful books.
To see our full range of titles, please visit our website at
www.wakefieldpress.com.au.

Wakefield Press thanks Fox Creek Wines
and Arts South Australia for their support.